Whitewater Tales of Terror

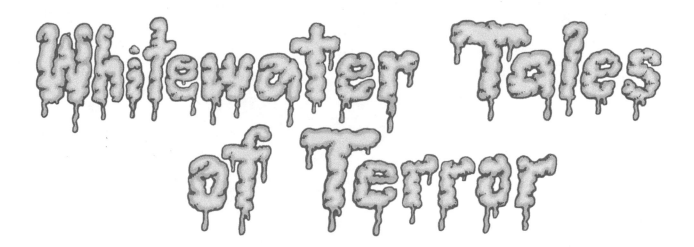

William Nealy

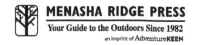

MENASHA RIDGE PRESS
Your Guide to the Outdoors Since 1982
an imprint of AdventureKEEN

Whitewater Tales of Terror

Printed in the United States of America

Published by
MENASHA RIDGE PRESS
Your Guide to the Outdoors Since 1982
an imprint of AdventureKEEN

2204 First Ave. S., Ste. 102
Birmingham, Alabama 35233
800-678-7006, FAX 877-374-9016
adventurewithkeen.com

ISBN 978-1-63404-372-4 (pbk); ISBN 978-1-63404-373-1 (ebook)

PUBLISHER'S NOTE

What you hold in your hands is a book of William Nealy's art, pulled from the gnarliest Class VI rapids of time . . . almost lost forever.

But now Nealy's zany illustrations have been bound and bandaged together in a new monumental collection, including books and cartoons long out of print. Nealy's full-speed downhill no-holds-barred art has been reset and brought back to life like never before.

This is the craziest collection of cartoons since Nealy first put paddle to water and pen to paper. The result is a hilarious slice of the outdoor community as extreme and cutting as Nealy was himself.

Many of the illustrations have not been seen since they were first published. Now they're back and will certainly delight old and new Nealy fans alike. We've taken care to make sure the flow of Nealy's stories and illustrations work just as well in this new format as they did when they were first published years ago.

We are proud at Menasha Ridge Press and AdventureKEEN to help return Nealy's art and irreverent illustrations to the bookshelf. Nealy had a gift for teaching, storytelling, and capturing the beauty of the rivers he sketched and the people he loved. His humorous approach to telling the twisted tales of paddlers, mountain bikers, hikers, campers, inline skaters, and skiers everywhere is a gift to all participating in the weird, wonderful world of outdoor sports.

You can learn more about William, his art, and his many books at thewilliamnealy.com.

SINCERELY,
THE MENASHA RIDGE
PRESS TEAM

This book is dedicated to the three Dans...

Big Dan

Young Dan

Little Dan

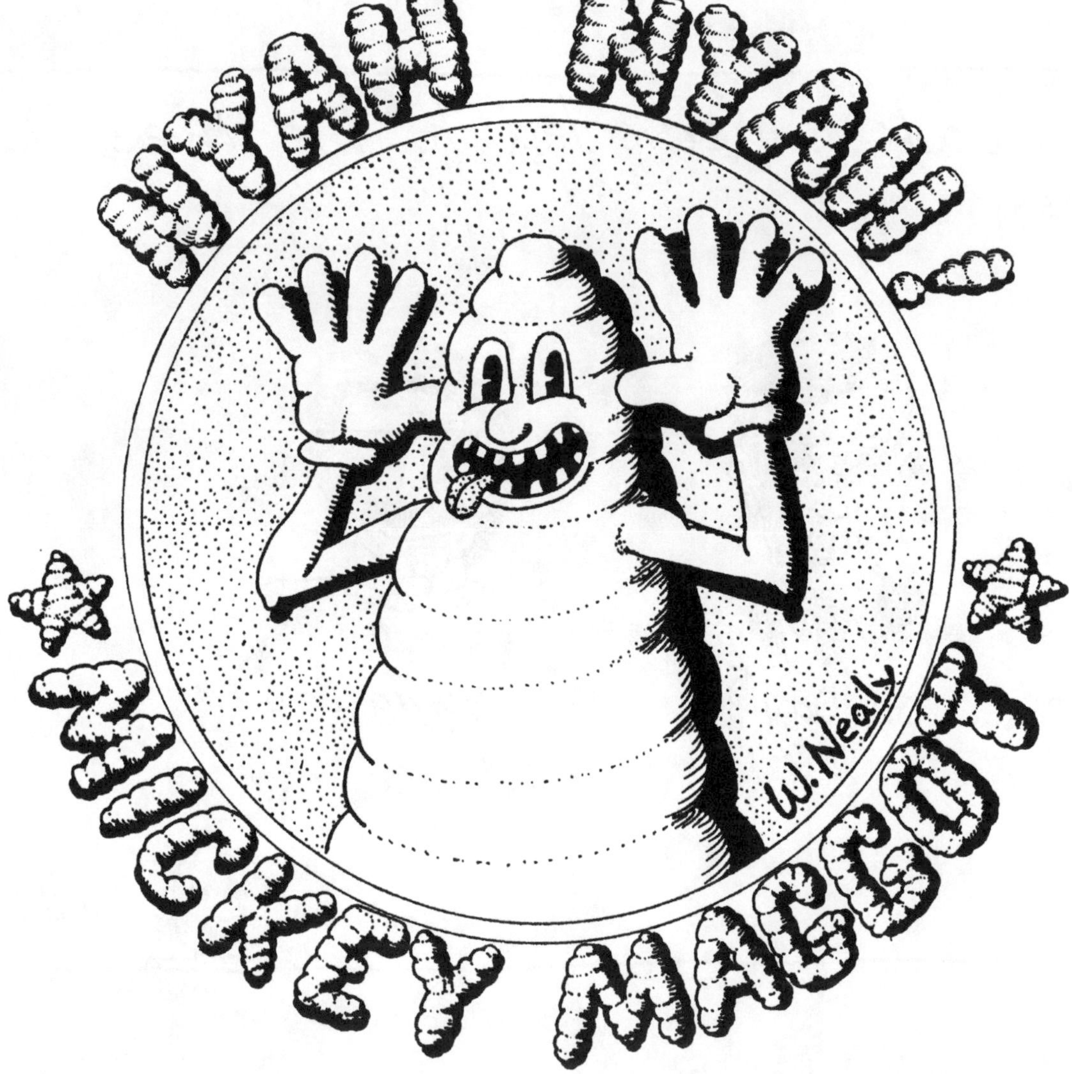
NYAH NYAH!
MICKEY MAGGOT
W. Nealy

Acknowledgements....

First of all I'd like to thank a few people for their kind assistance, comic inspiration, and psychic life-support... Mark Brown, Tam Fletcher, Tom Love, Holland "Is this all?" Wallace, Bob Miller, Cliff and Alice Earle, John Barbour, Don Banducci, Tom Schlinkert, Sarah Crichton, Guy Martin, John Regan, Class VI Riverrunners, Neal & Mothra Allen, Reg Lake, Haze Hanff, John Mills, Ester Szabo, Paul Thompson, Ed Gertler, Thrifty Outfitters, Charlie Walbridge, Terry Curtin, Aqua Pac, David Brown, Louise Nealy, Henry Unger, Bob & Alice Vernon, Friedrich Nietzsche, Bob Sehlinger, Frank Fleming, John Wassen, Tom Kruck, Bob, James & J.T, Bruce Hare, The Doobie Bros. (Not the band!), The Ramones (The band), Jim Perrigo, John Dragon, Mike Kinnard, Edgar Hitchcock, Ron Mace, Joan Wallace, Rangeley & Jim, Tracy Tiller, Barrie Wallace, Jim Screvin, Creative Printers, U-2, James Watt (thanks for the T-shirt royalties, Jim!), Glen Kovac, Doug Bush, Chance Danger, Bruce Tiller....

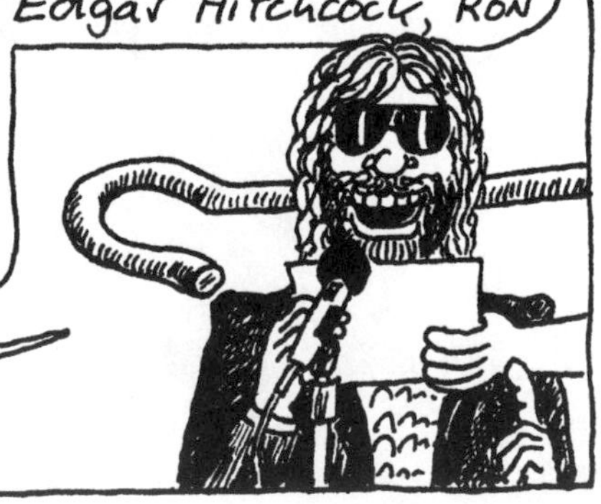

★ Back Cover Photo by Edgar Hitchcock ★

Fear of women is the basis of good health.

Spanish Proverb

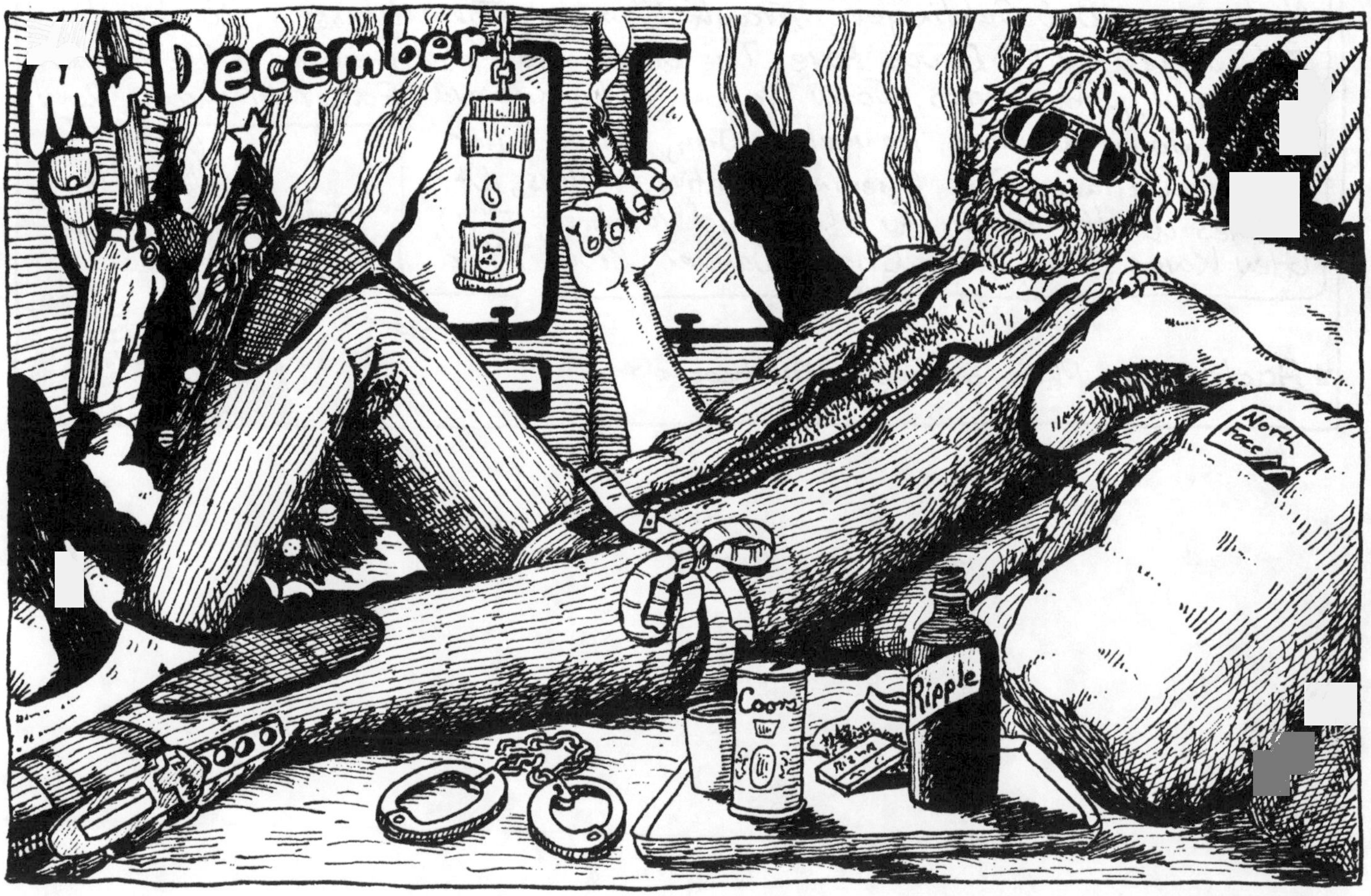
Mr. December
North Face
Coors
Ripple

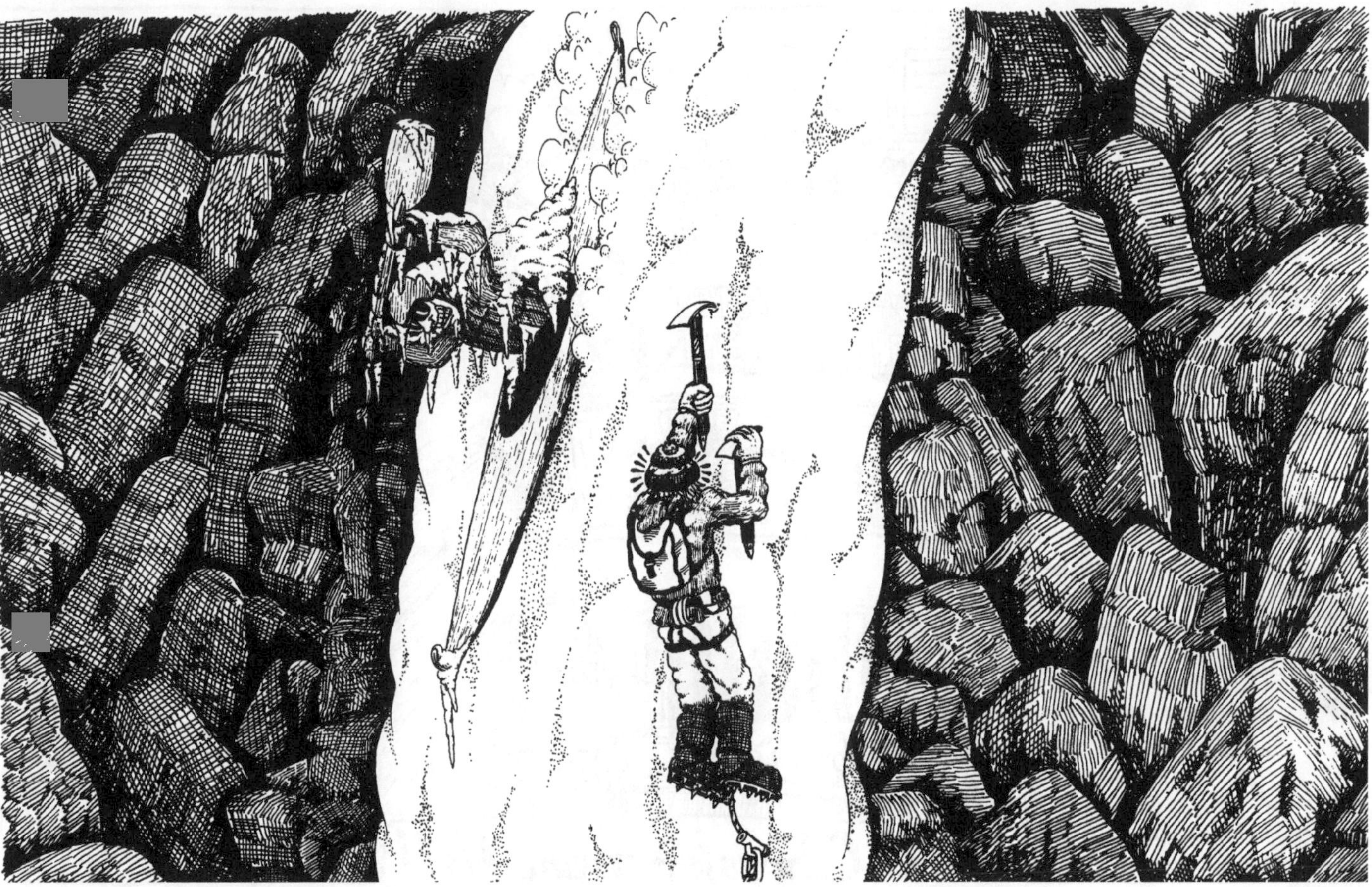

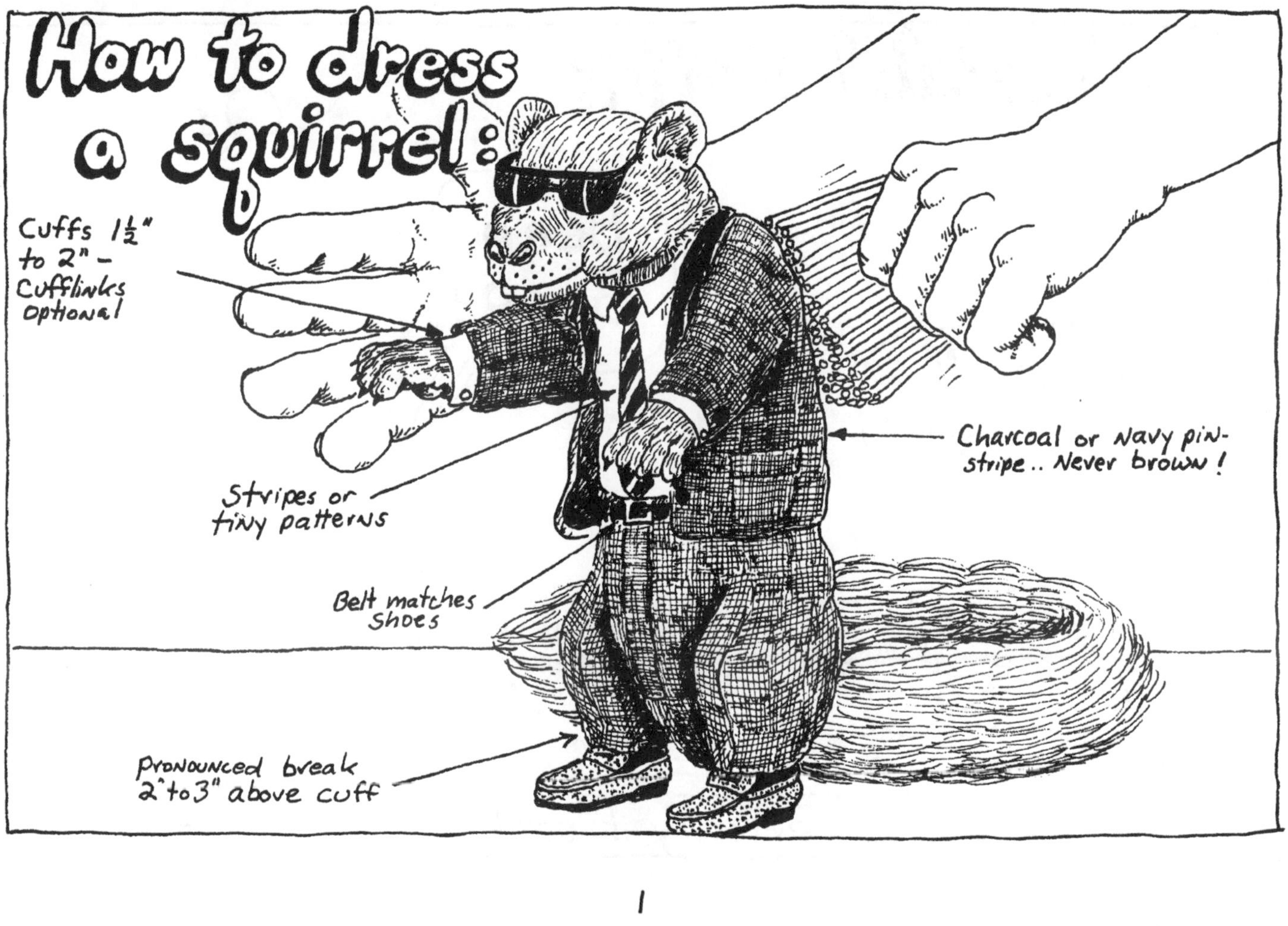
How to dress a squirrel:
Cuffs 1½" to 2" – Cufflinks optional
Stripes or tiny patterns
Belt matches shoes
Pronounced break 2" to 3" above cuff
Charcoal or Navy pin-stripe.. Never brown!

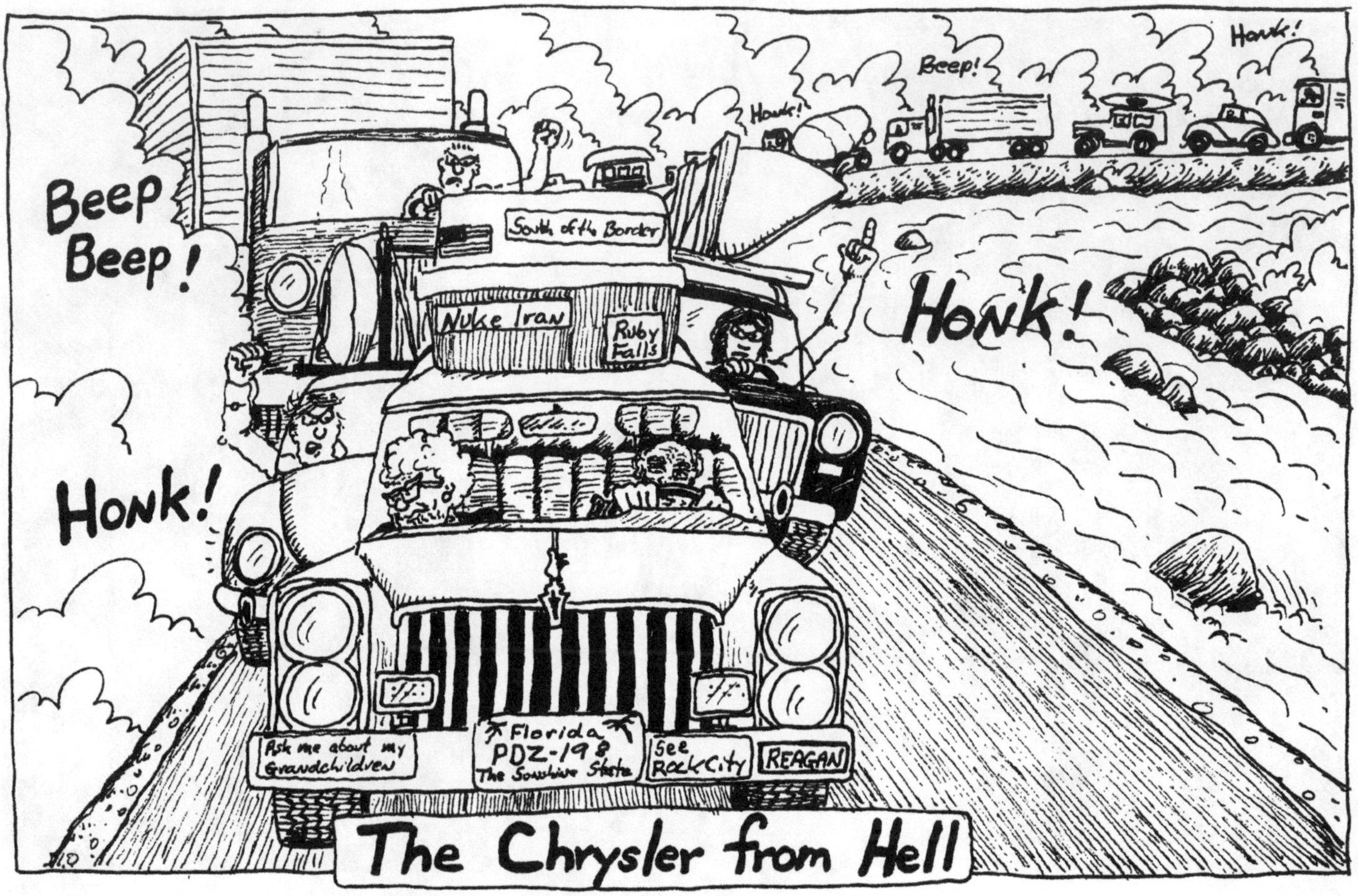
Beep Beep!
Honk!
Beep!
Honk!
Honk!
Beep Beep!
Honk!
South of the Border
Nuke Iran
Ruby Falls
Ask me about my Grandchildren
Florida
PDZ-198
The Sunshine State
See Rock City
REAGAN
The Chrysler from Hell

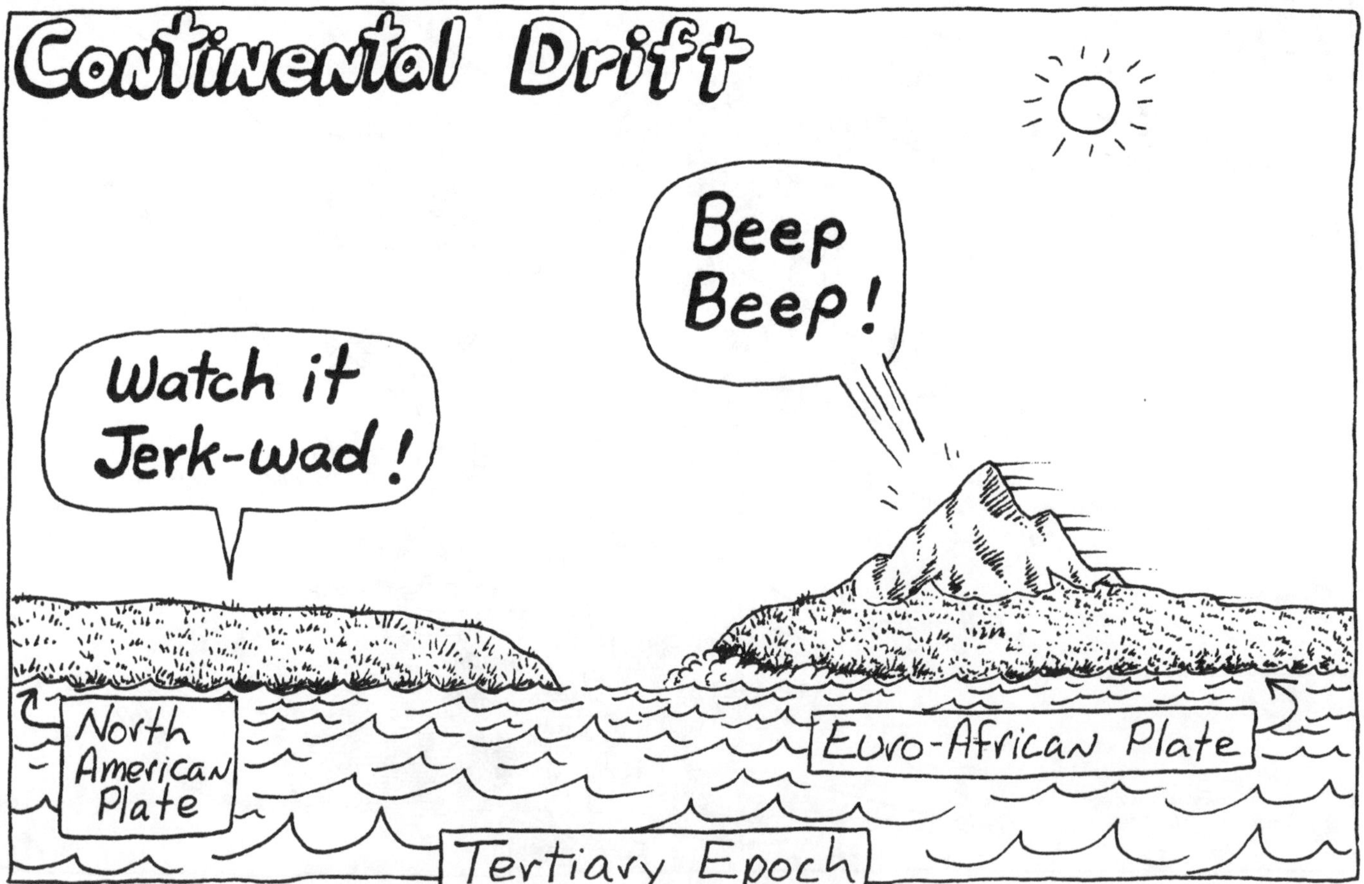
Continental Drift
Beep Beep!
Watch it Jerk-wad!
North American Plate
Euro-African Plate
Tertiary Epoch

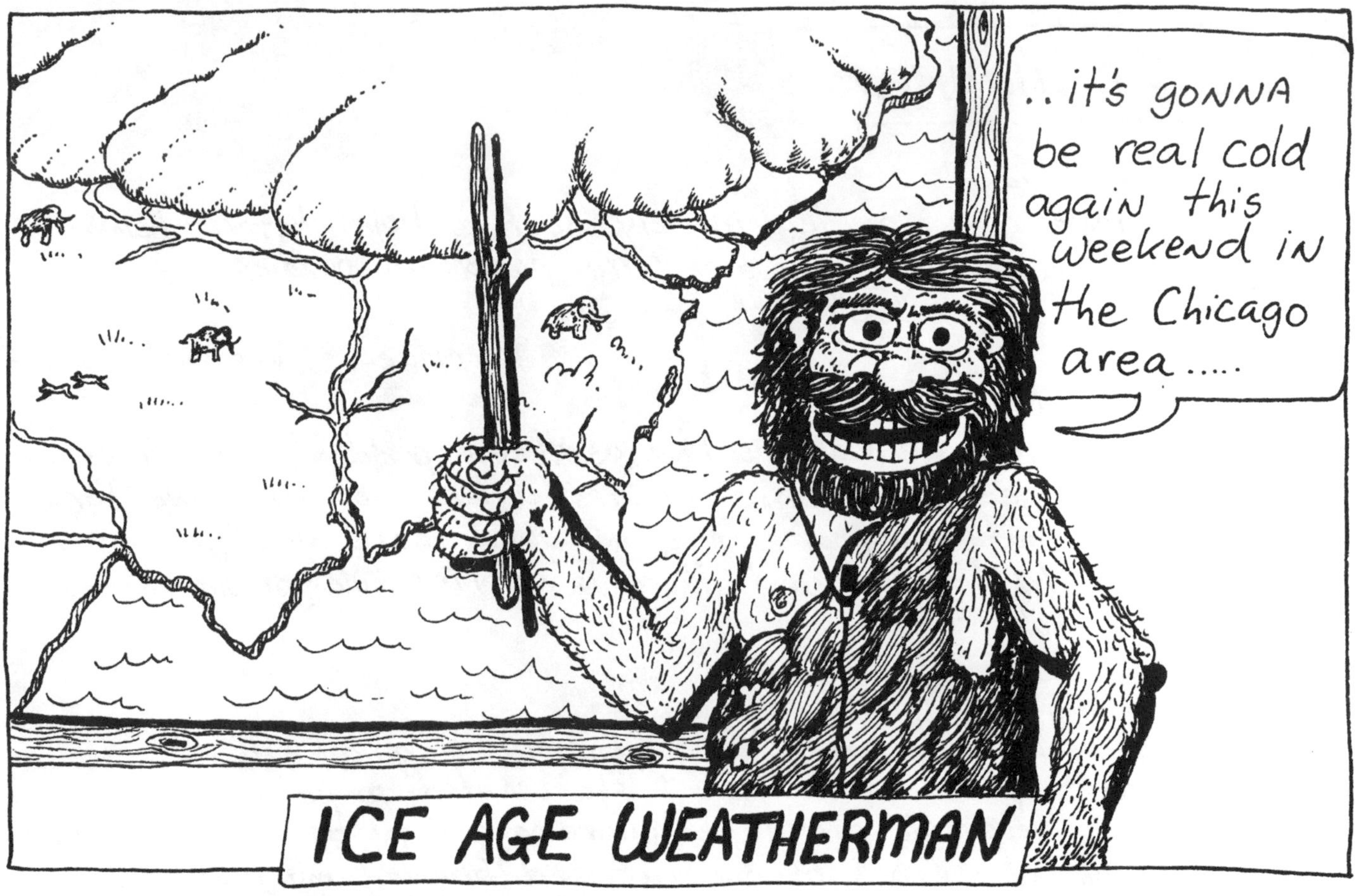
..it's GONNA be real cold again this weekend in the Chicago area.....
ICE AGE WEATHERMAN

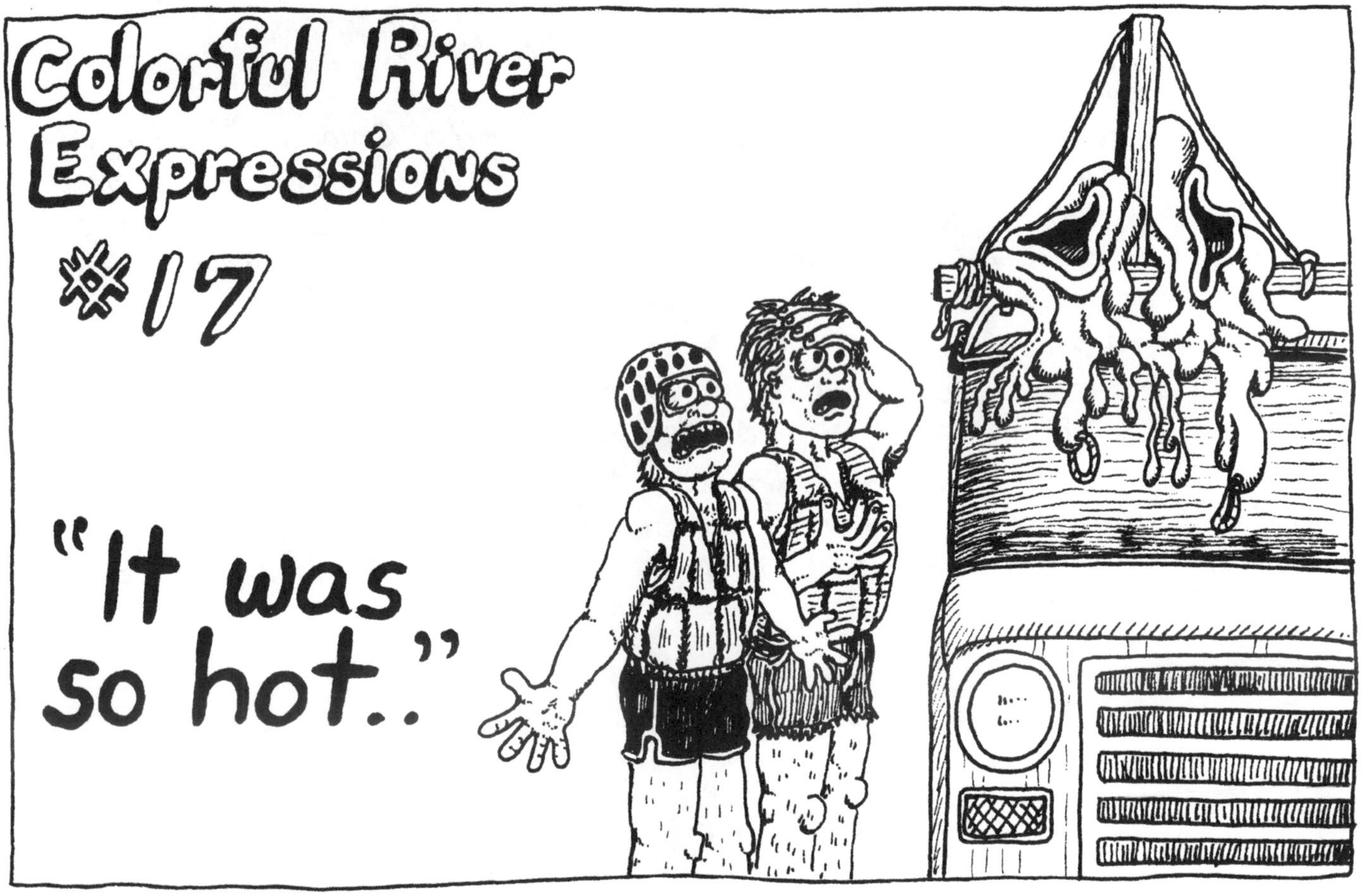
Colorful River Expressions
#17
"It was so hot.."

Ask Mr. Manners

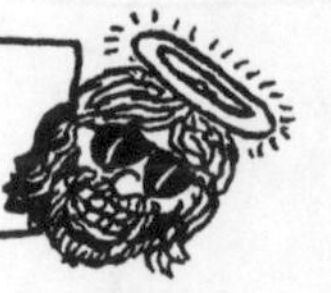

Dear Mr. Manners,

How long can you legitimately surf a hole before being called a "hole hog" or worse? My paddling buddies say two minutes is the rule. What do you say?

Perplexed

Dear Perplexed,

Your buddies are right as long as they're paddling in the Southeast. Out West the general rule is 3 minutes unless you are posing for advertising or magazine photographs, in which case you get an extra minute. In the MidWest there is no time rule, providing you can find a hole to surf.

Dear Mr. Manners,

Last weekend I saw this gorgeous chick guiding a raft. I paddled right up and asked her if she wanted to party later on. Here's the unbelievable part; she hammered a 5 gal. bailing bucket over my head, pulled me out of my boat, and 'binered my jock strap to a "D" ring and dragged me through a nasty rapid before letting me go! Chicks tell me I look like Tom Selleck, so what gives?

Frustrated

Dear Frustrated,

Did you forget to mention your "dynamite Colombo"? Consider yourself lucky to be alive. She probably had a negative reaction to your approach, which I gather is none too subtile. Next time pretend you have dislocated your elbow and appeal to her maternal instincts. Keep your mouth shut except to breathe.

Dear Mr. Manners,

If you eddy out in a rapid and find yourself breaking in line to surf a hole do you have to go to the end of the line? Ed (my paddling partner) says you <u>can</u> break in line only during the initial running of the rapid as long as your intent was to eddy out to rest or scout, not to surf. Does Ed's doctrine of malicious intent apply on the river?

Confused in Ohio

Dear Ohio,

Go to the end of the line. Good luck to your buddy Ed.

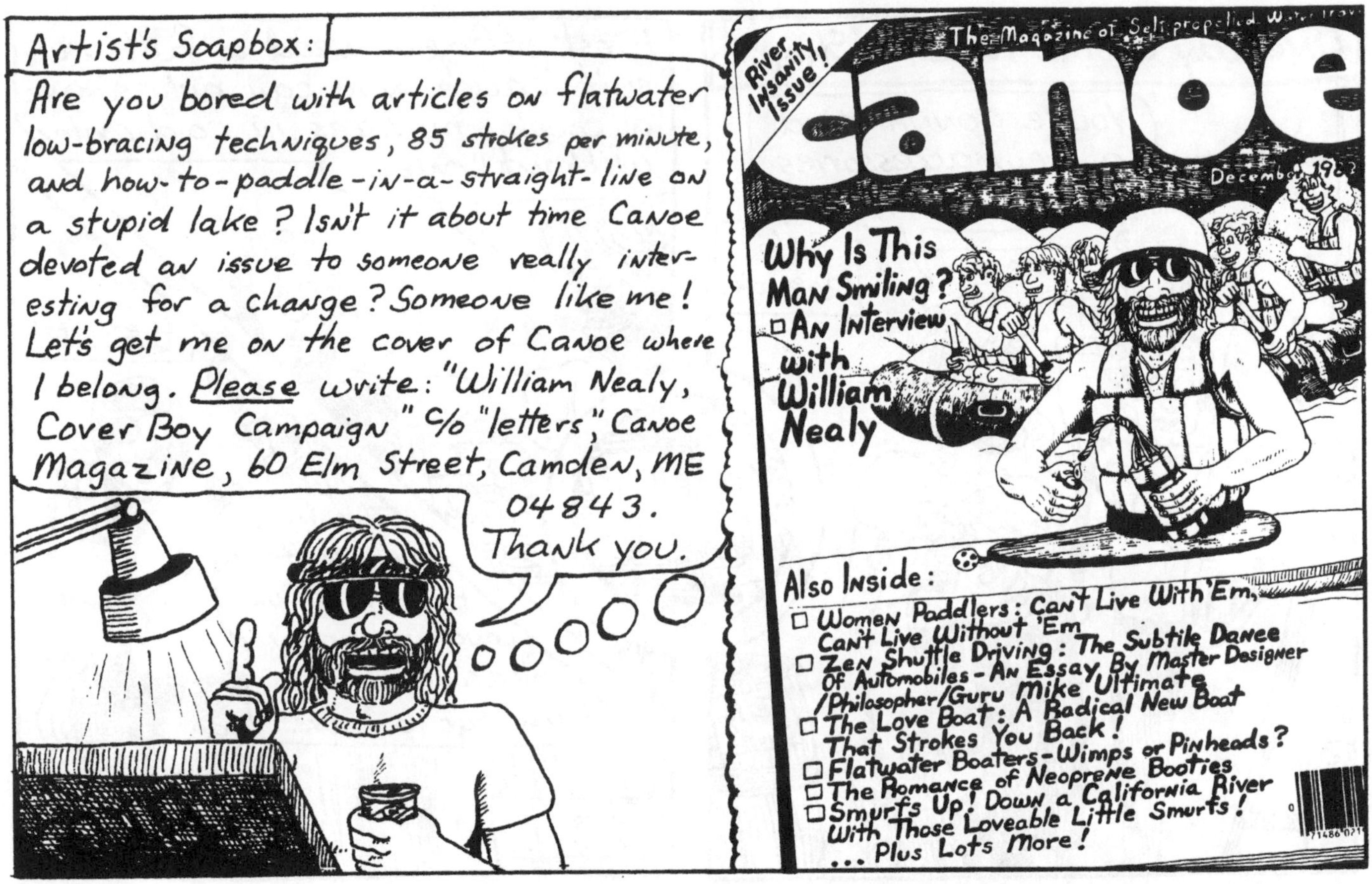
Artist's Soapbox:
Are you bored with articles on flatwater low-bracing techniques, 85 strokes per minute, and how-to-paddle-in-a-straight-line on a stupid lake? Isn't it about time Canoe devoted an issue to someone really interesting for a change? Someone like me! Let's get me on the cover of Canoe where I belong. Please write: "William Nealy, Cover Boy Campaign" c/o "letters," Canoe Magazine, 60 Elm Street, Camden, ME 04843. Thank you.
River Insanity Issue!
The Magazine of Self-propelled
canoe
December
Why Is This Man Smiling?
□ An Interview with William Nealy
Also Inside:
□ Women Paddlers: Can't Live With 'Em, Can't Live Without 'Em
□ Zen Shuttle Driving: The Subtile Dance Of Automobiles - An Essay By Master Designer /Philosopher/Guru Mike Ultimate
□ The Love Boat: A Radical New Boat That Strokes You Back!
□ Flatwater Boaters - Wimps or Pinheads?
□ The Romance of Neoprene Booties
□ Smurfs Up! Down a California River With Those Loveable Little Smurfs!
... Plus Lots More!

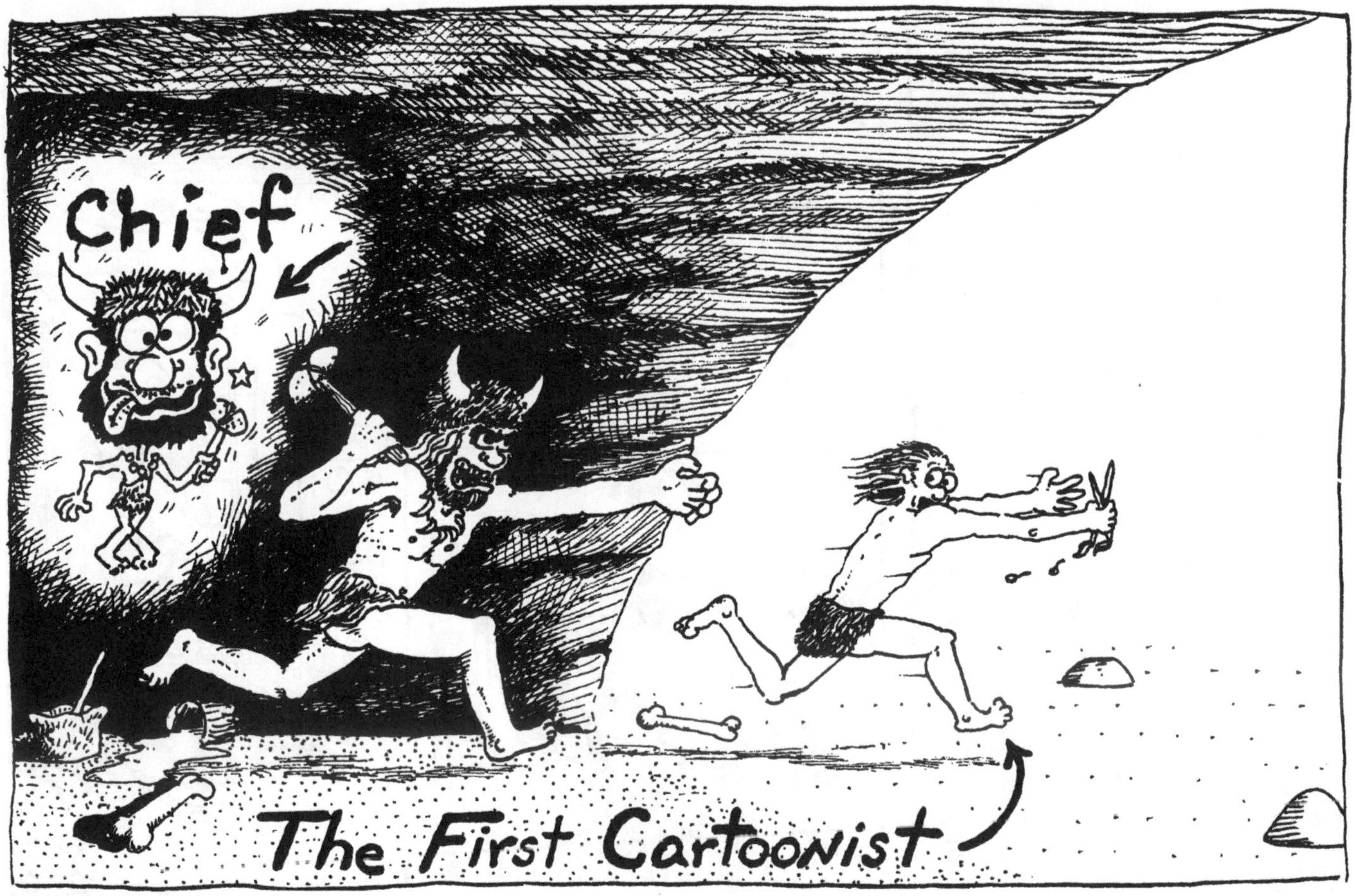
Chief
The First Cartoonist

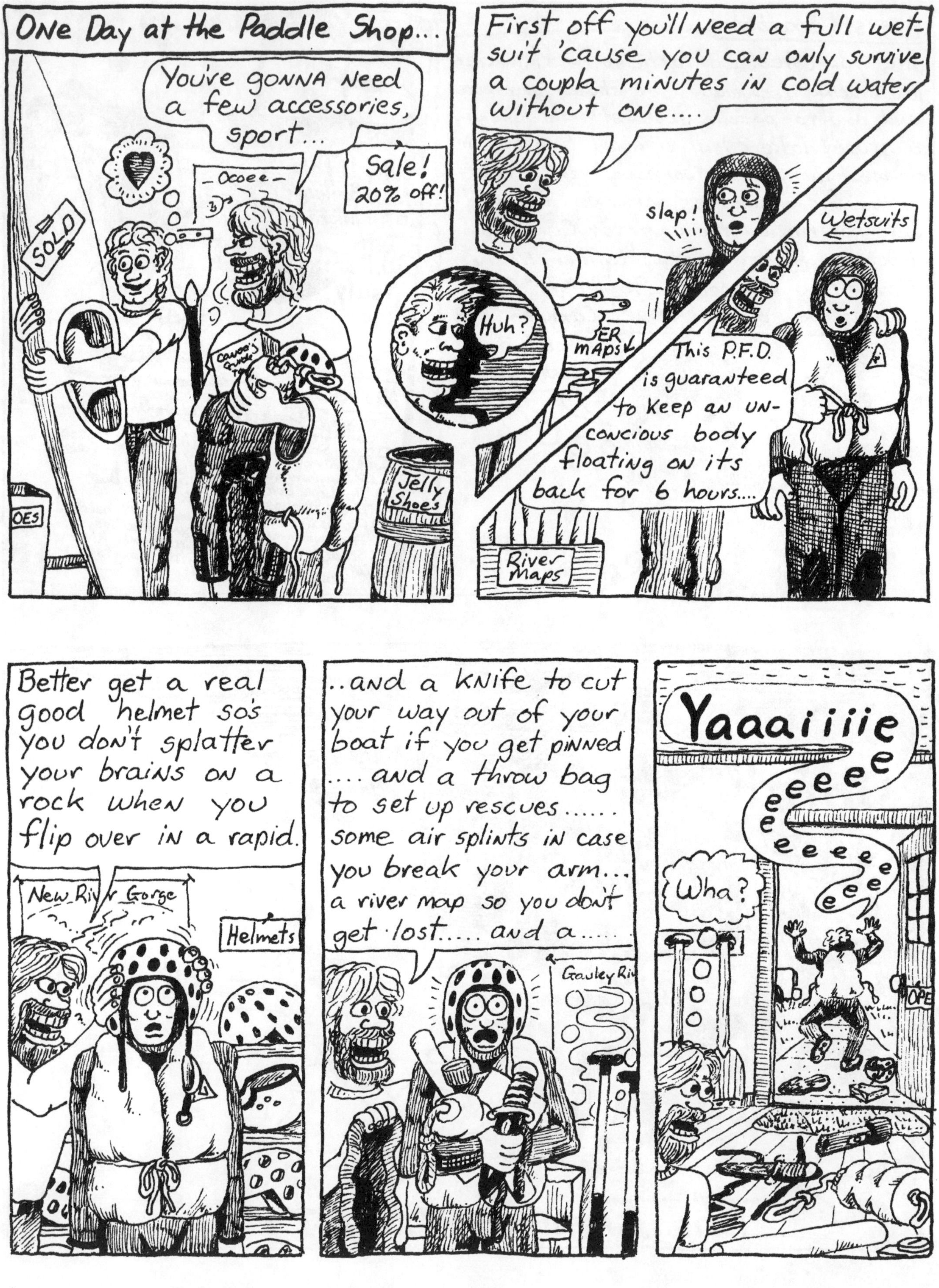
One Day at the Paddle Shop...
You're gonna need a few accessories, sport...
Sale! 20% off!
-Ocoee-
SOLD
Jelly Shoes
Huh?
First off you'll need a full wet-suit 'cause you can only survive a coupla minutes in cold water without one....
slap!
Wetsuits
This P.F.D. is guaranteed to keep an un-concious body floating on its back for 6 hours....
River Maps
Better get a real good helmet so's you don't splatter your brains on a rock when you flip over in a rapid.
New River Gorge
Helmets
..and a knife to cut your way out of your boat if you get pinned .... and a throw bag to set up rescues..... some air splints in case you break your arm... a river map so you don't get lost.... and a....
Gauley Riv
Yaaaiiiie eeeeeeeeeeeeee
Wha?

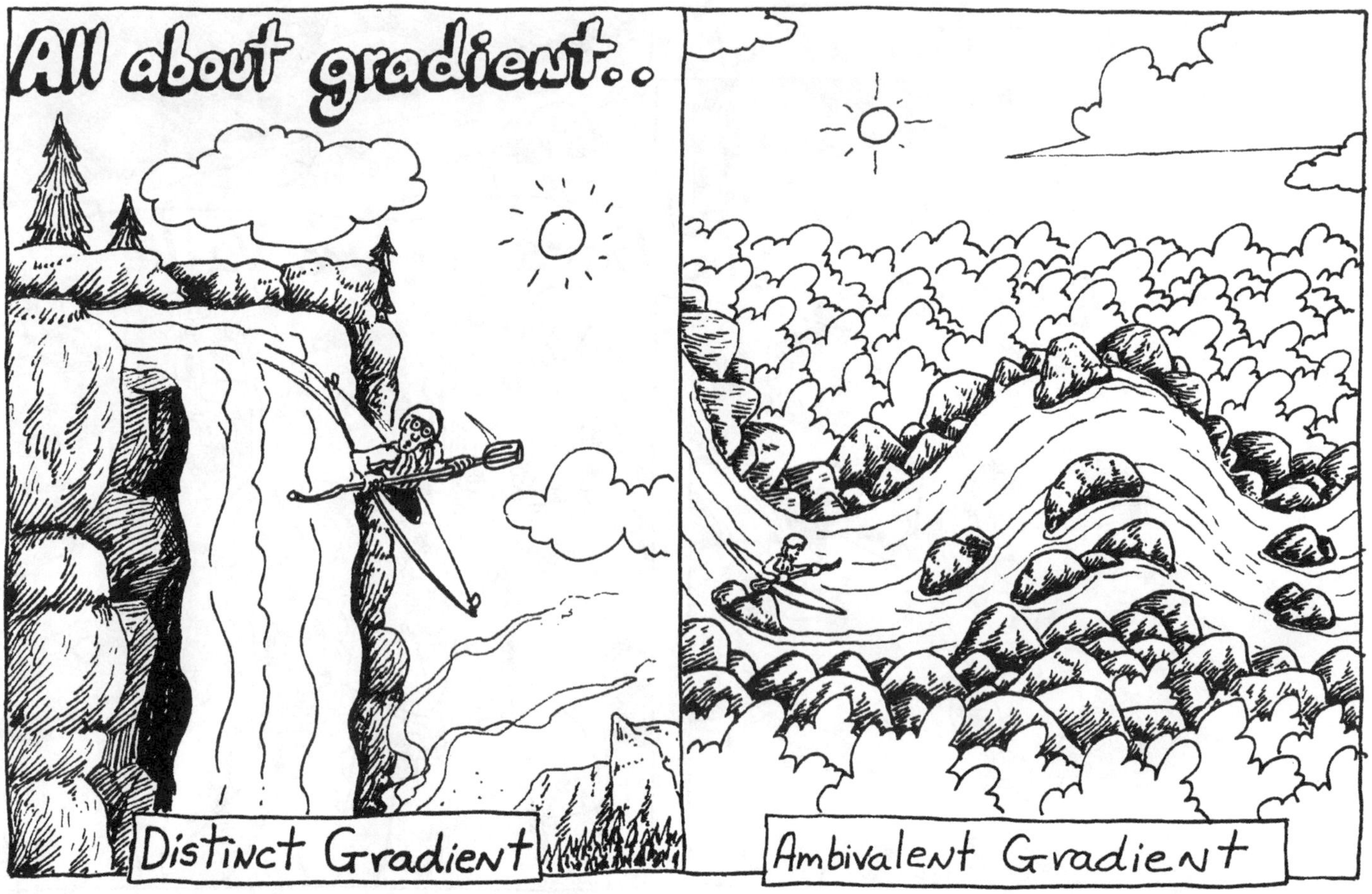
All about gradient..
Distinct Gradient
Ambivalent Gradient

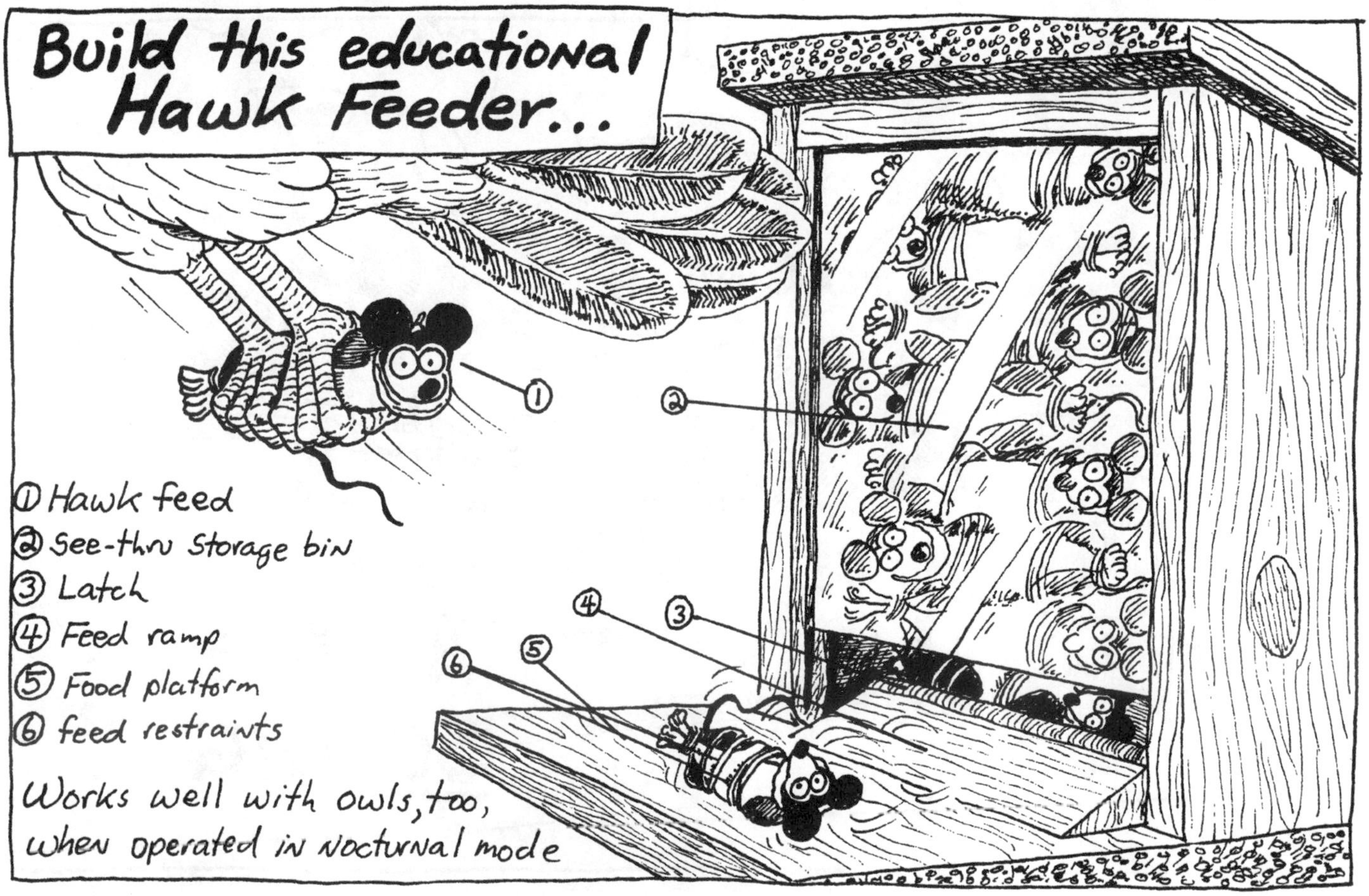
Build this educational Hawk Feeder...
① Hawk feed
② See-thru storage bin
③ Latch
④ Feed ramp
⑤ Food platform
⑥ feed restraints
Works well with owls, too, when operated in nocturnal mode
①
②
③
④
⑤
⑥

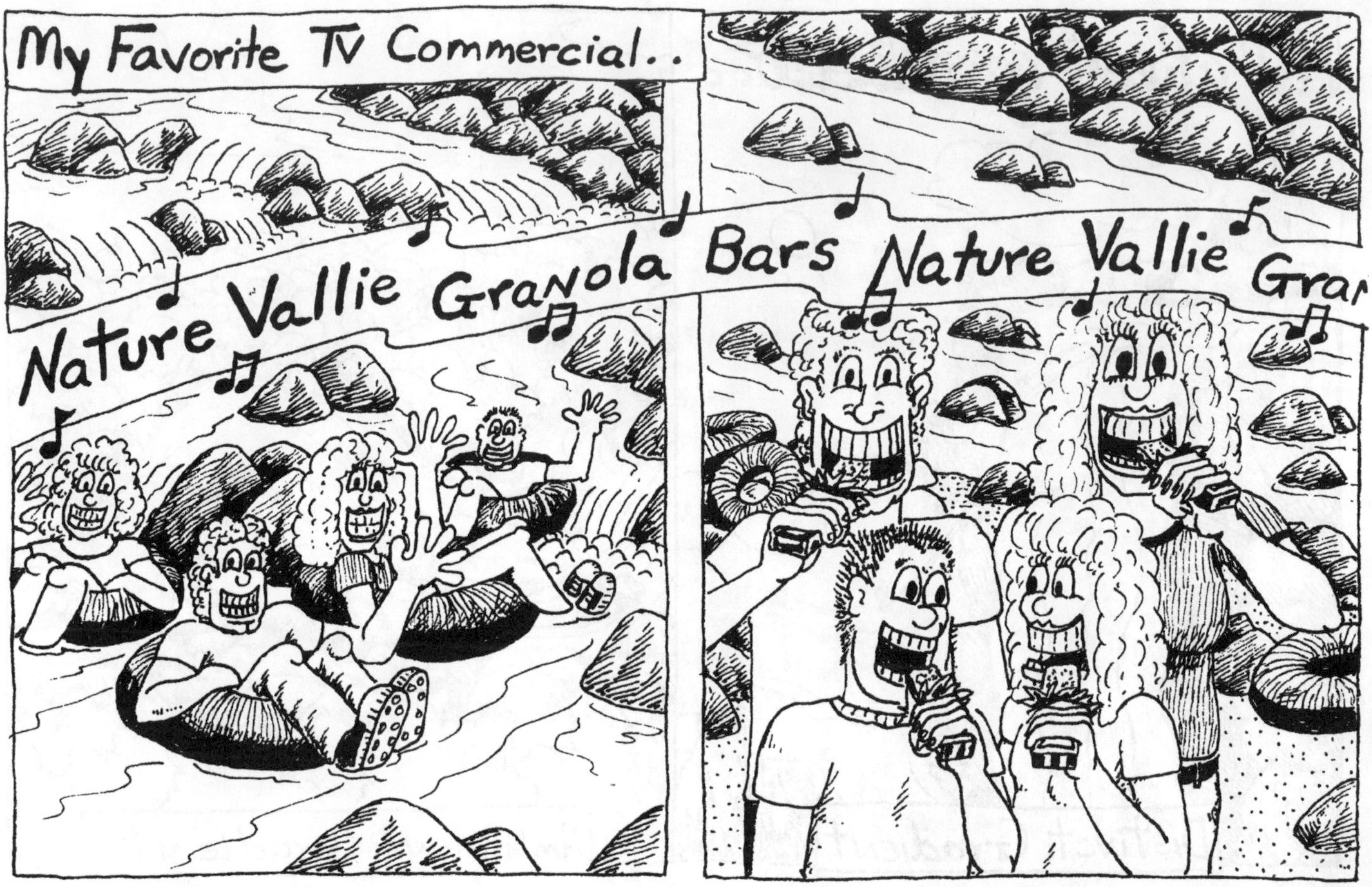
My Favorite TV Commercial..
Nature Vallie Granola Bars Nature Vallie Gran

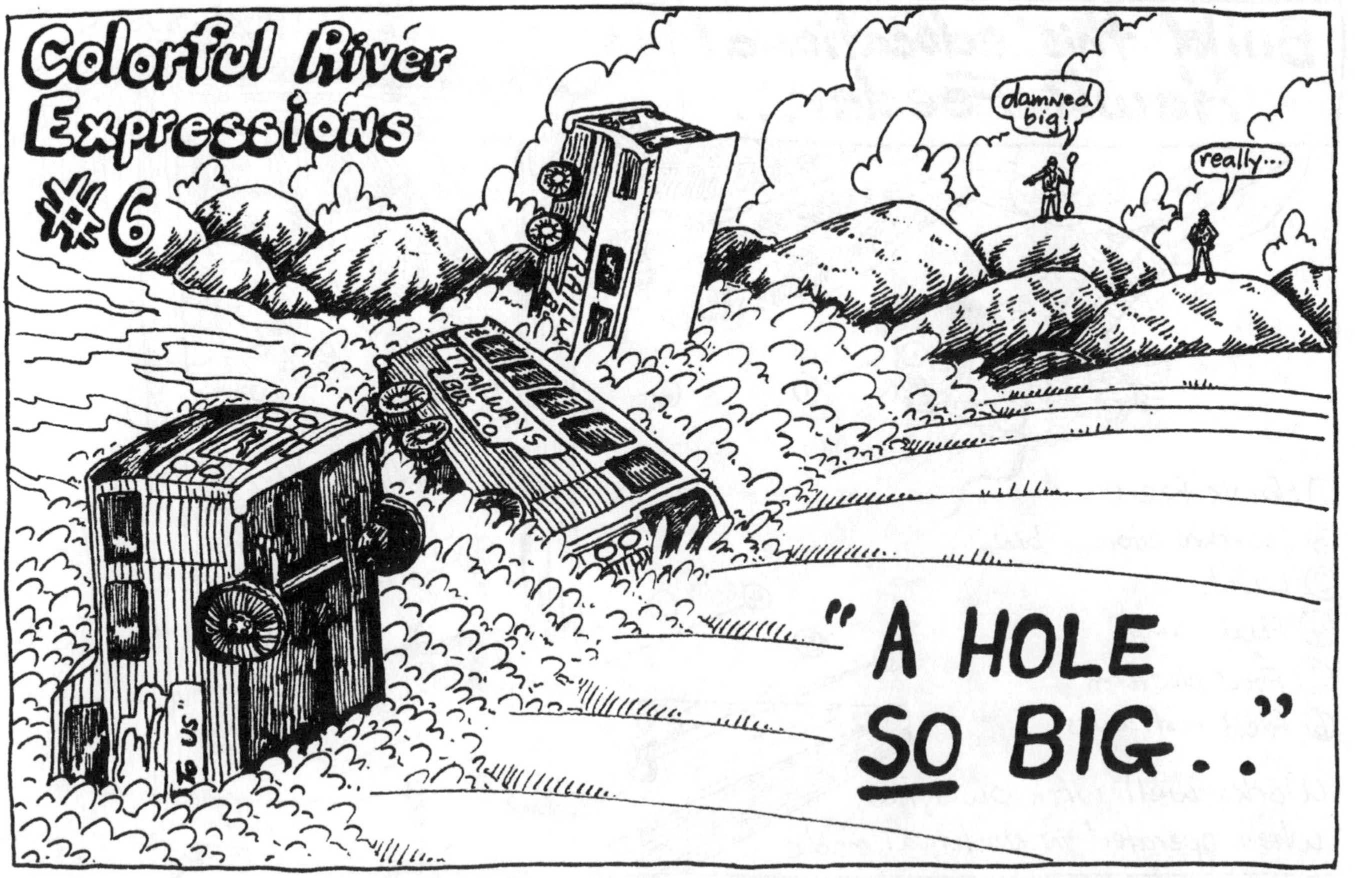
Colorful River Expressions #6
damned big!
really...
TRAILWAYS BUS CO
"A HOLE SO BIG.."

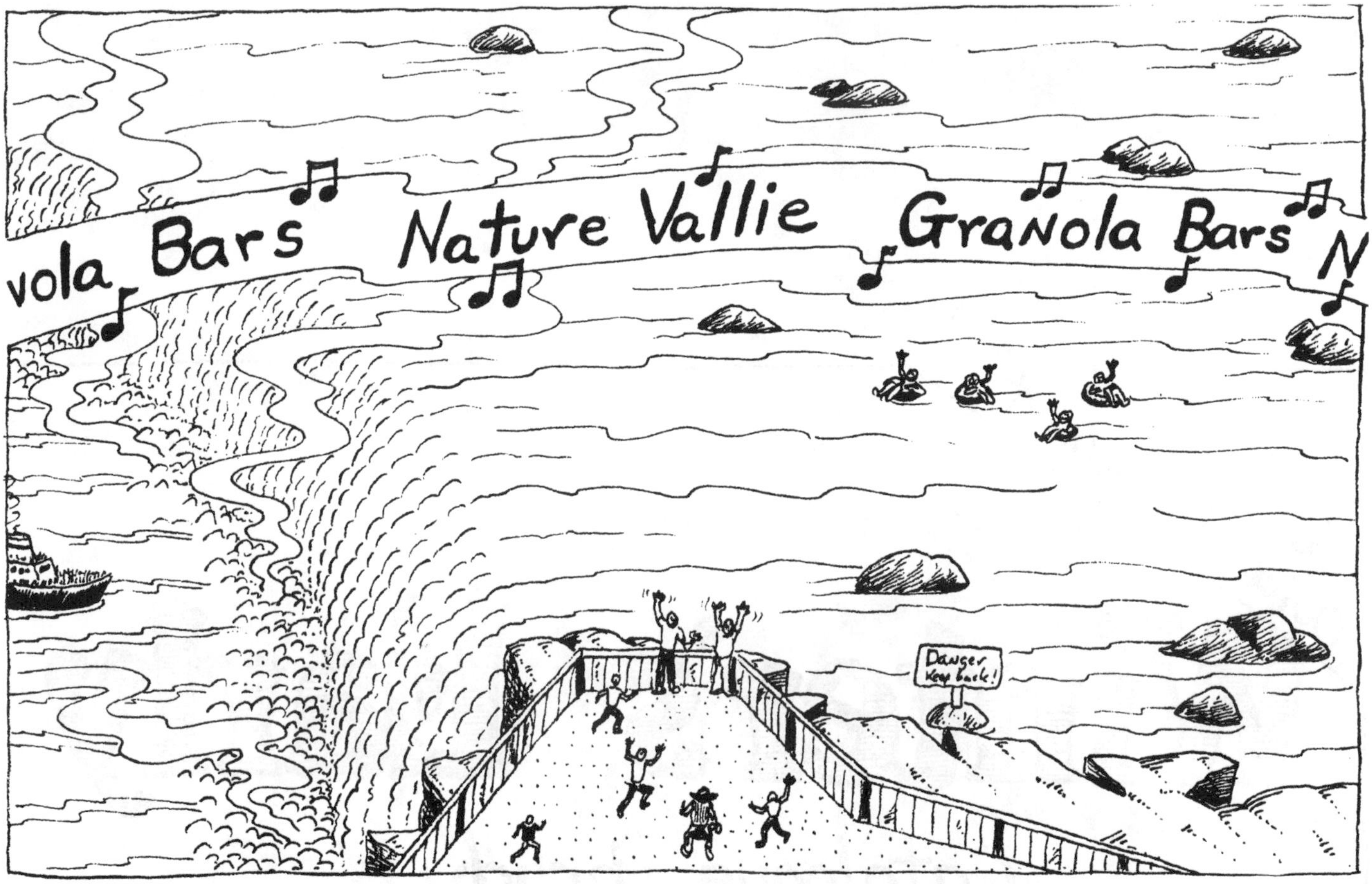
vola Bars Nature Vallie Granola Bars N
Danger Keep back!

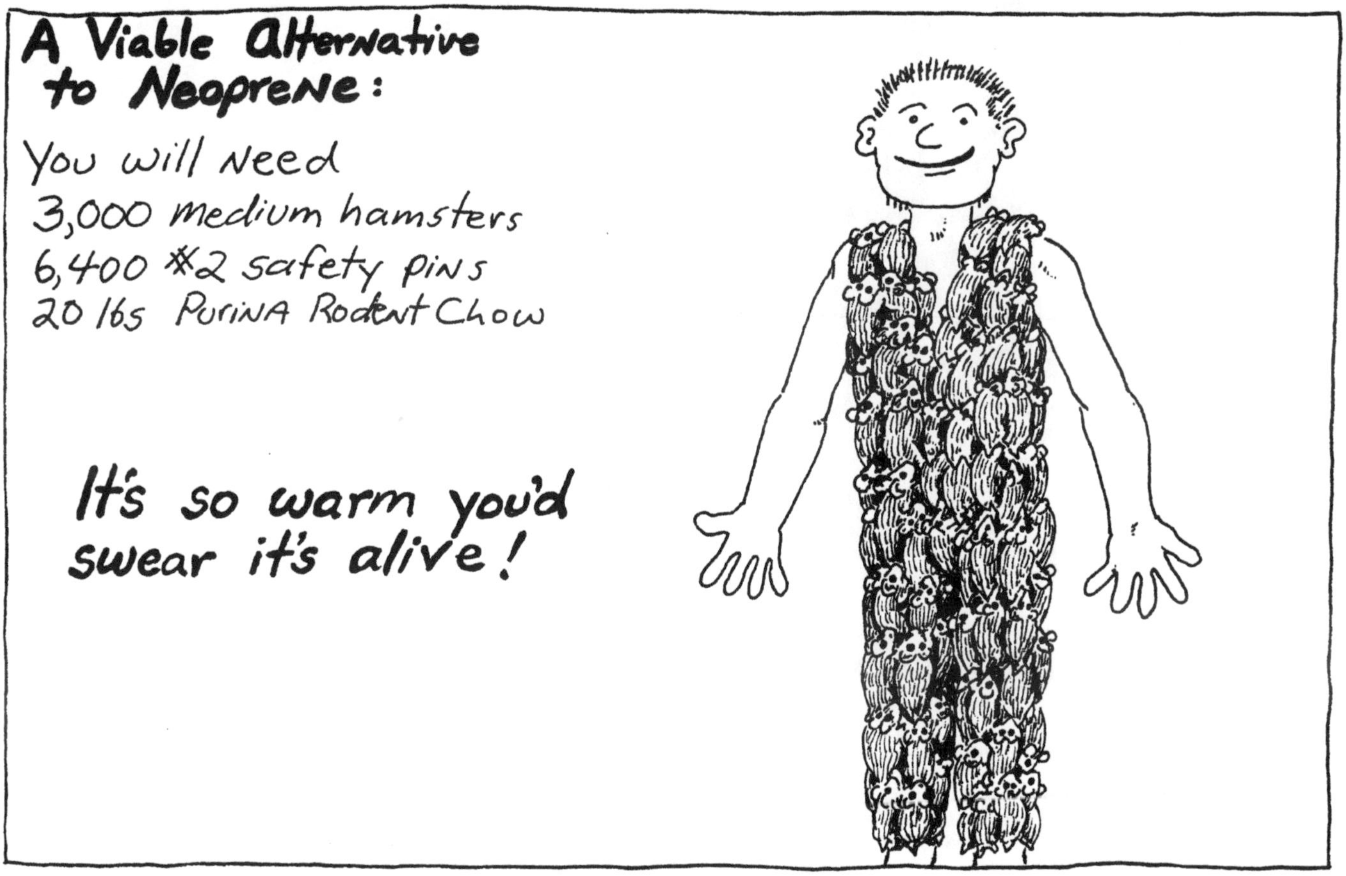
A Viable Alternative to Neoprene:
You will need
3,000 medium hamsters
6,400 #2 safety pins
20 lbs Purina Rodent Chow
It's so warm you'd swear it's alive!

Unique Outdoor Equipment

Winter's Early

Catalogue Parody

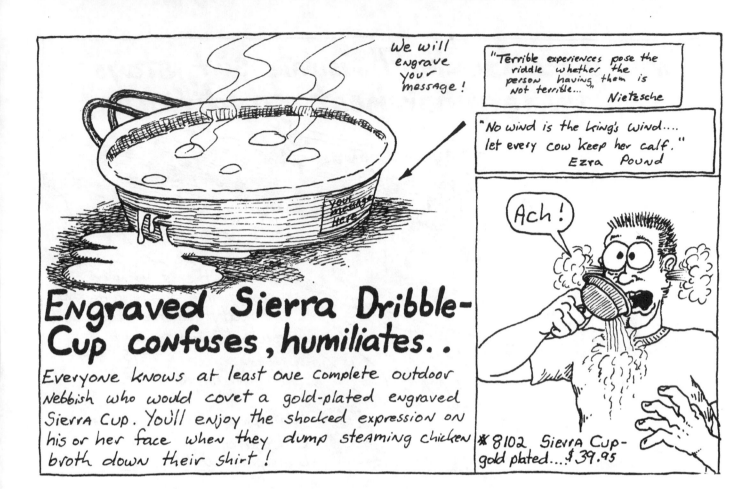

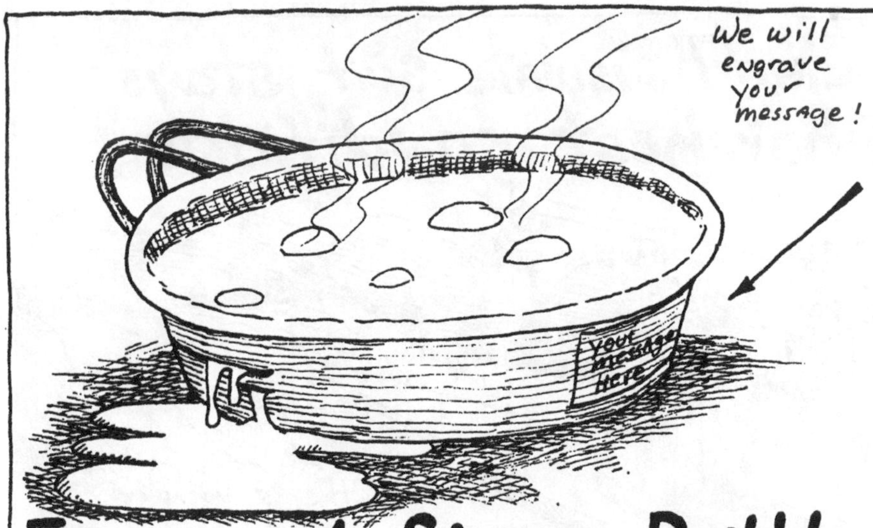
We will engrave your message!
Your message Here

"Terrible experiences pose the riddle whether the person having them is not terrible..." Nietzsche

"No wind is the king's wind.... let every cow keep her calf." Ezra Pound

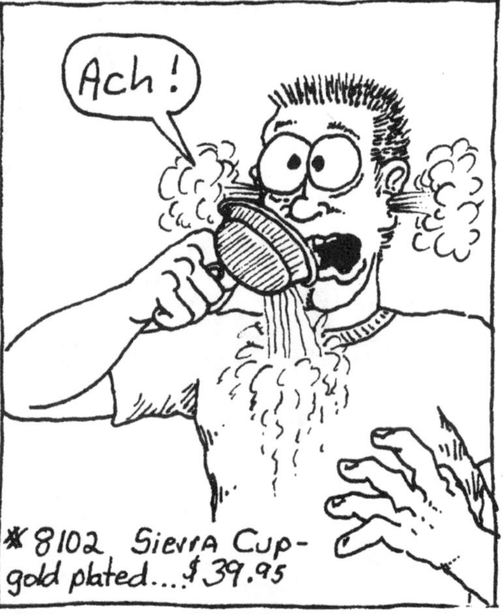
Ach!

Engraved Sierra Dribble-Cup confuses, humiliates..

Everyone knows at least one complete outdoor Nebbish who would covet a gold-plated engraved Sierra Cup. You'll enjoy the shocked expression on his or her face when they dump steaming chicken broth down their shirt!

*8102 Sierra Cup-gold plated....$39.95

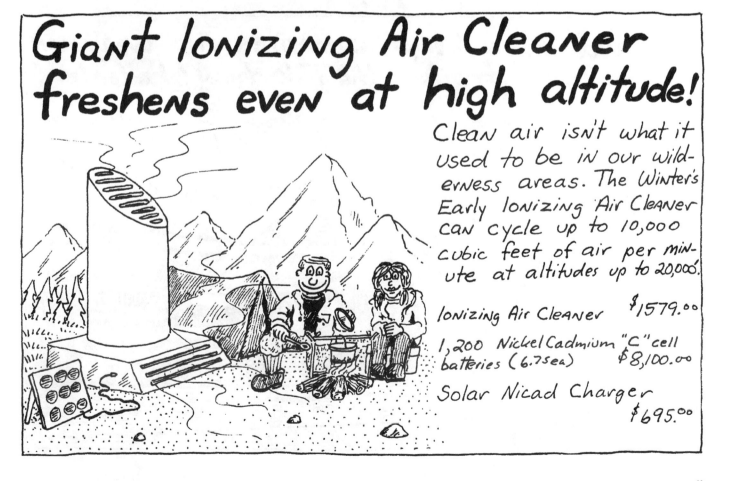

Giant Ionizing Air Cleaner freshens even at high altitude!

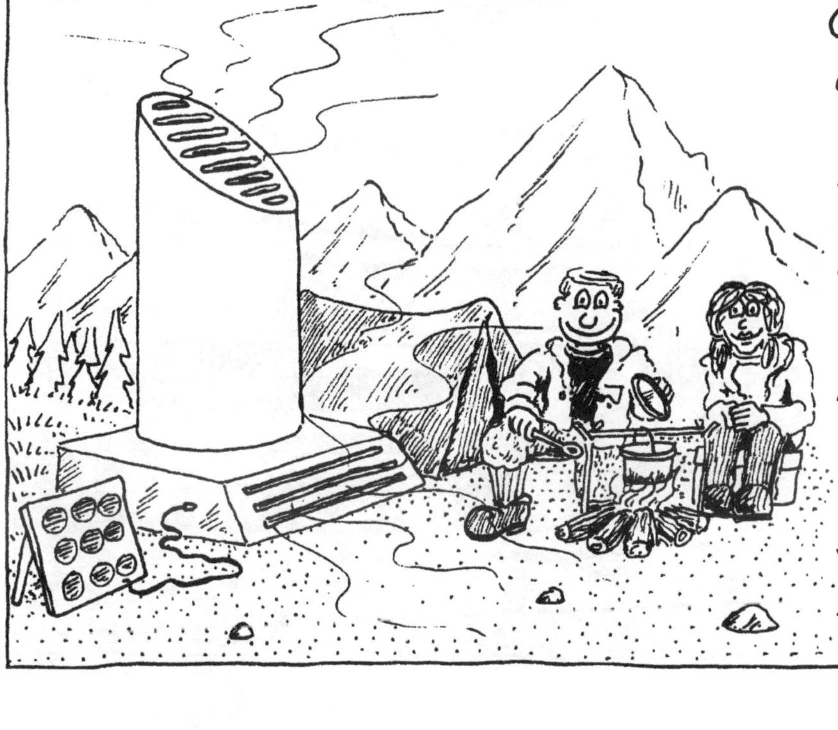

Clean air isn't what it used to be in our wilderness areas. The Winter's Early Ionizing Air Cleaner can cycle up to 10,000 cubic feet of air per minute at altitudes up to 20,000'.

Ionizing Air Cleaner $1579.00

1,200 Nickel Cadmium "C" cell batteries (6.75 ea) $8,100.00

Solar Nicad Charger $695.00

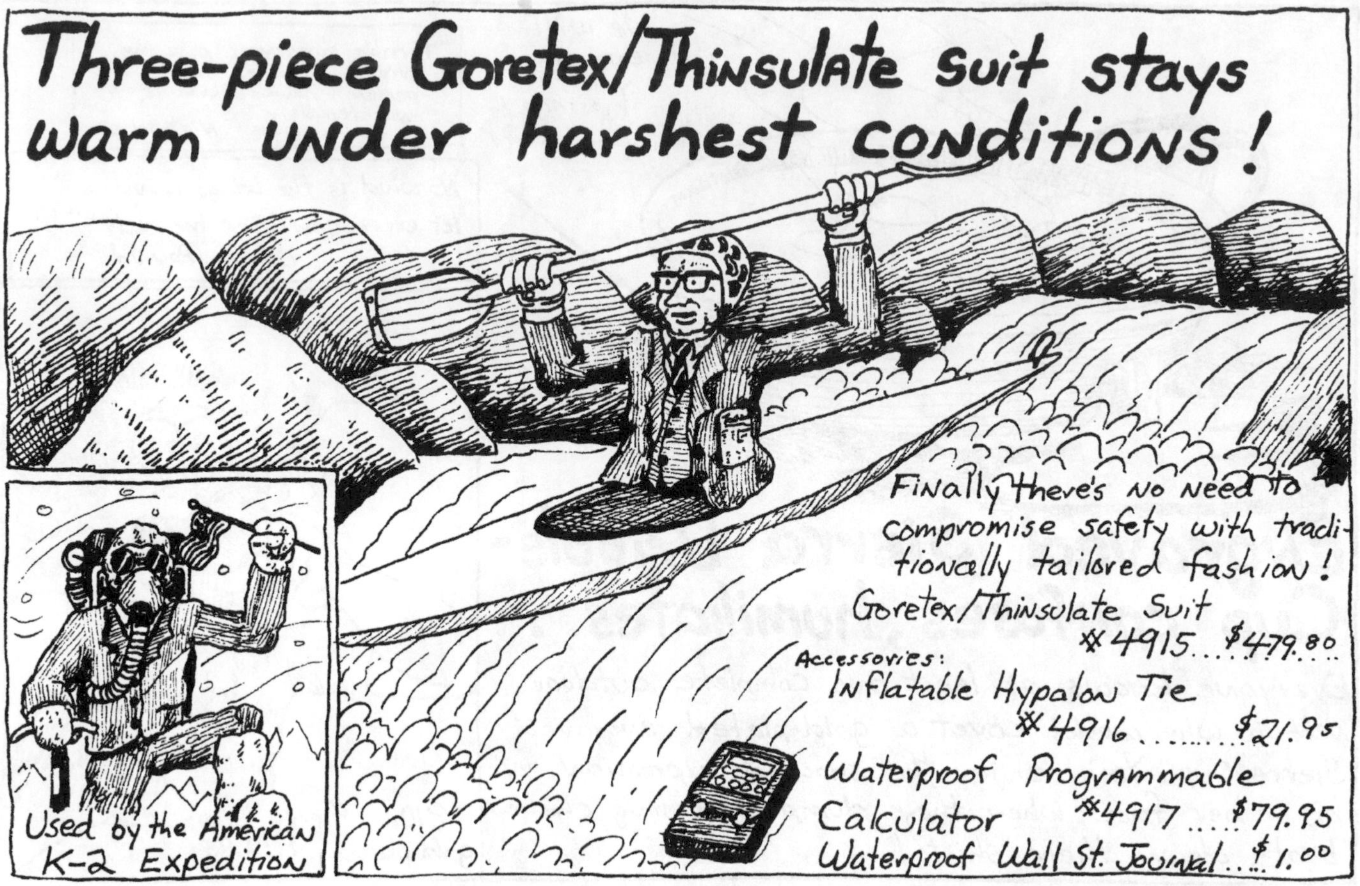
Three-piece Goretex/Thinsulate suit stays warm under harshest conditions!
Used by the American K-2 Expedition
Finally there's no need to compromise safety with traditionally tailored fashion!
Goretex/Thinsulate Suit
#4915....$479.80
Accessories:
Inflatable Hypalon Tie
#4916..........$21.95
Waterproof Programmable Calculator #4917....$79.95
Waterproof Wall St. Journal....$1.00

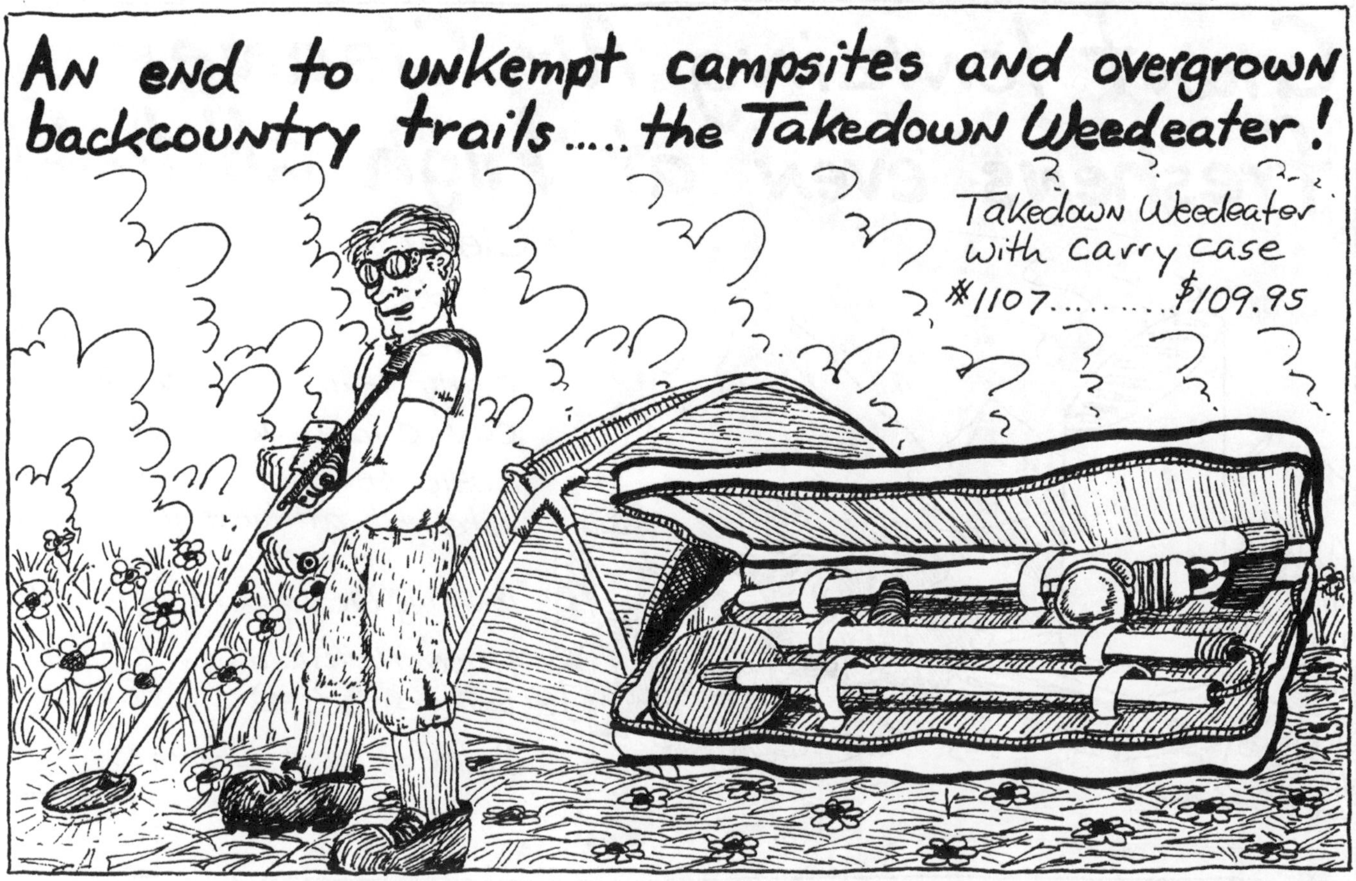
An end to unkempt campsites and overgrown backcountry trails..... the Takedown Weedeater!
Takedown Weedeater with carry case
#1107.........$109.95

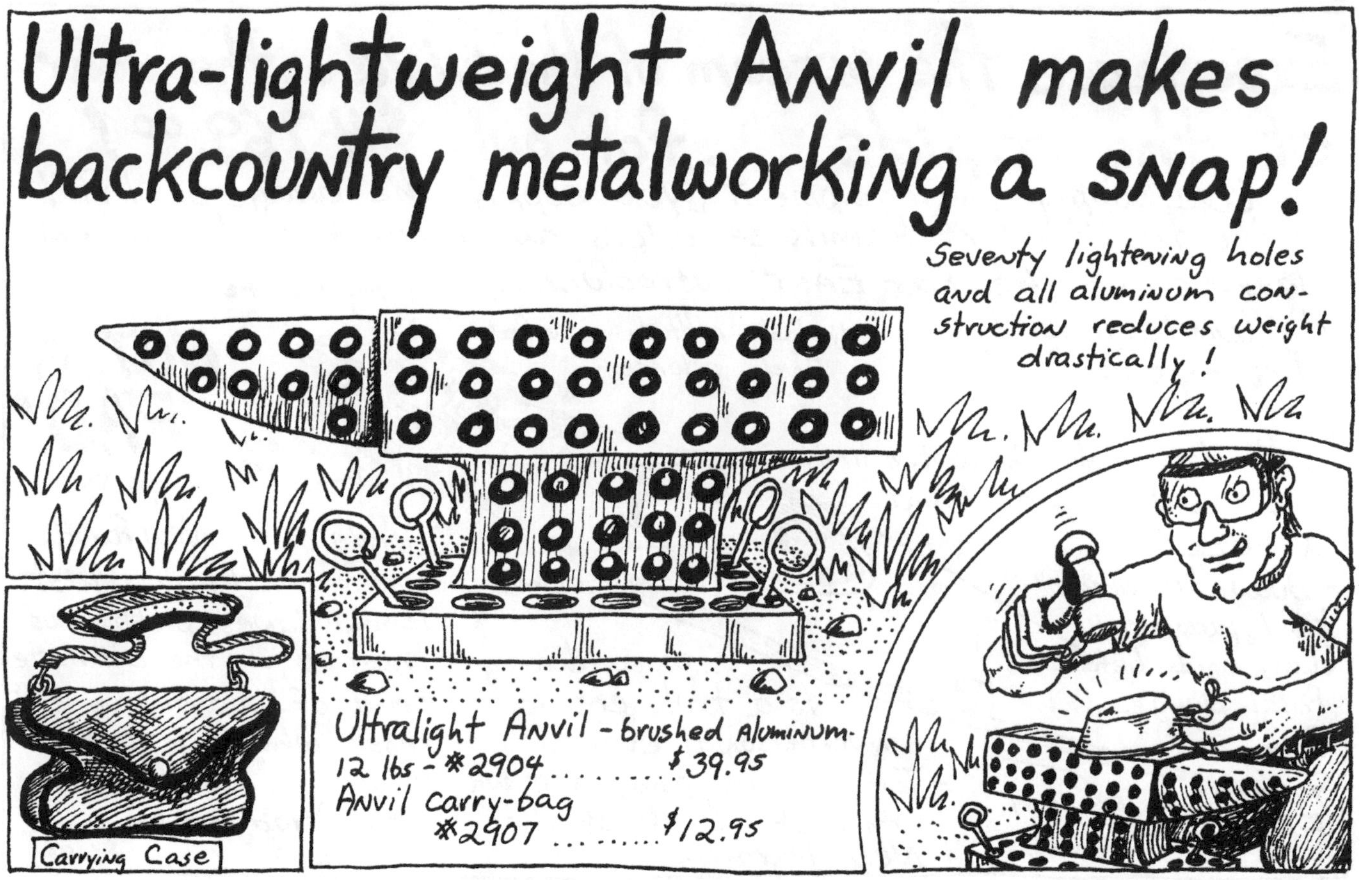
Ultra-lightweight Anvil makes backcountry metalworking a snap!
Seventy lightening holes and all aluminum construction reduces weight drastically!
Carrying Case
Ultralight Anvil - brushed Aluminum - 12 lbs - #2904 .... $39.95
Anvil carry-bag #2907 .... $12.95

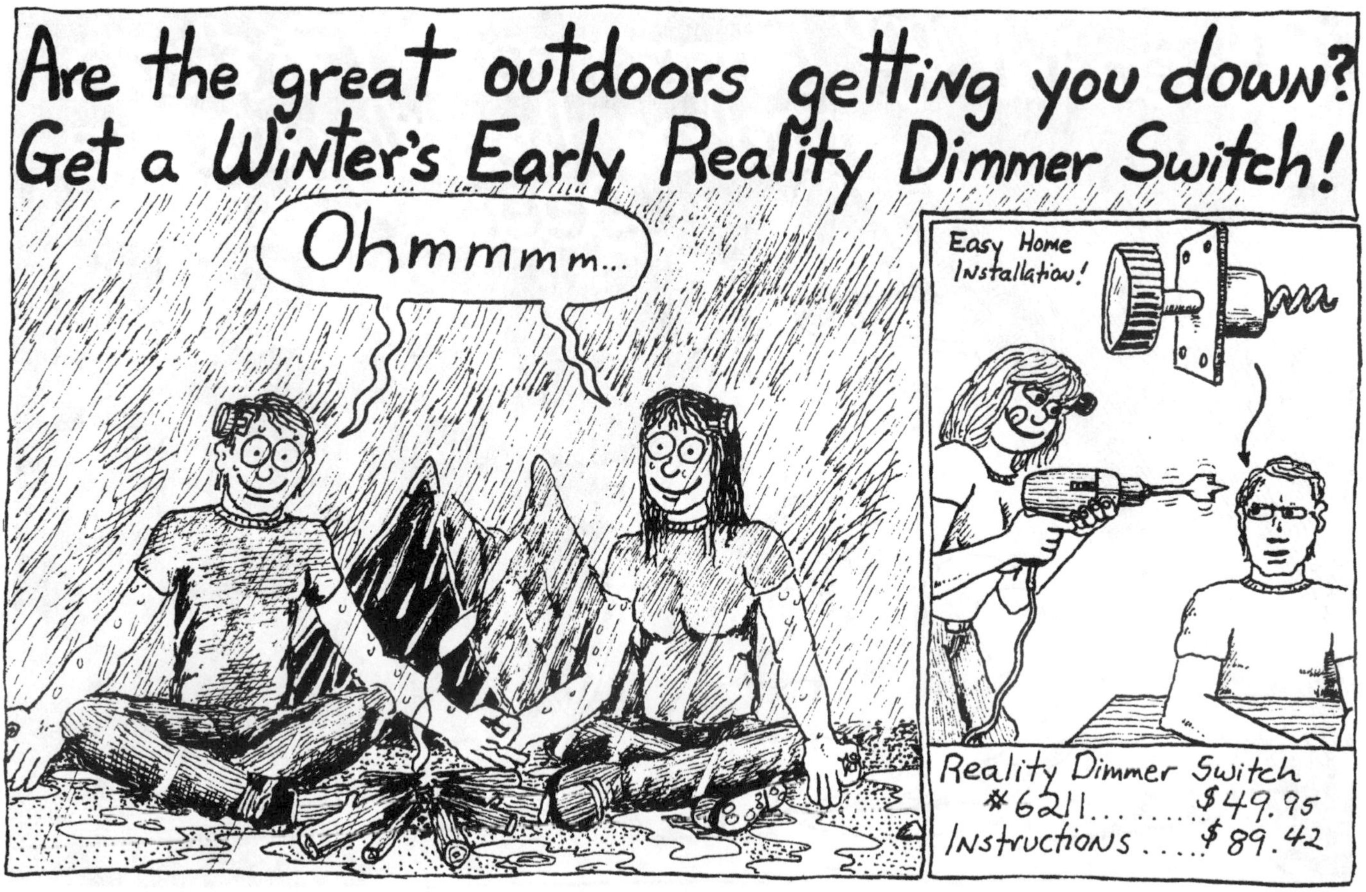
Are the great outdoors getting you down? Get a Winter's Early Reality Dimmer Switch!
Ohmmmm...
Easy Home Installation!
Reality Dimmer Switch #6211........ $49.95
Instructions.... $89.42

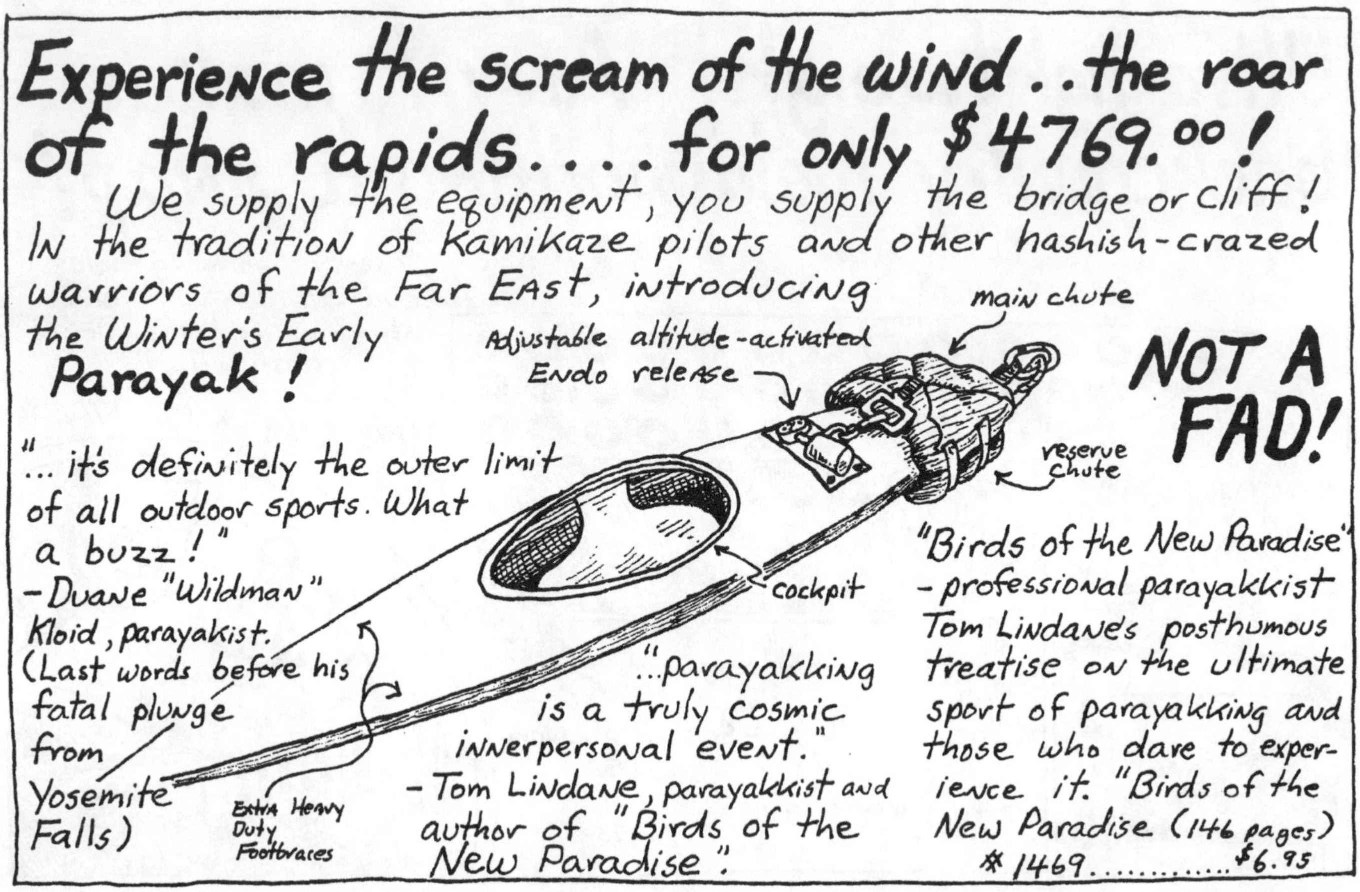
Experience the scream of the wind .. the roar of the rapids.... for only $4769.00!
We supply the equipment, you supply the bridge or cliff! In the tradition of Kamikaze pilots and other hashish-crazed warriors of the Far East, introducing the Winter's Early
Parayak!
Adjustable altitude-activated Endo release
main chute
NOT A FAD!
reserve chute
cockpit
"... it's definitely the outer limit of all outdoor sports. What a buzz!" -Duane "Wildman" Kloid, parayakist. (Last words before his fatal plunge from Yosemite Falls)
Extra Heavy Duty Footbraces
"...parayakking is a truly cosmic innerpersonal event." - Tom Lindane, parayakkist and author of "Birds of the New Paradise".
"Birds of the New Paradise" - professional parayakkist Tom Lindane's posthumous treatise on the ultimate sport of parayakking and those who dare to experience it. "Birds of the New Paradise (146 pages) #1469............$6.95

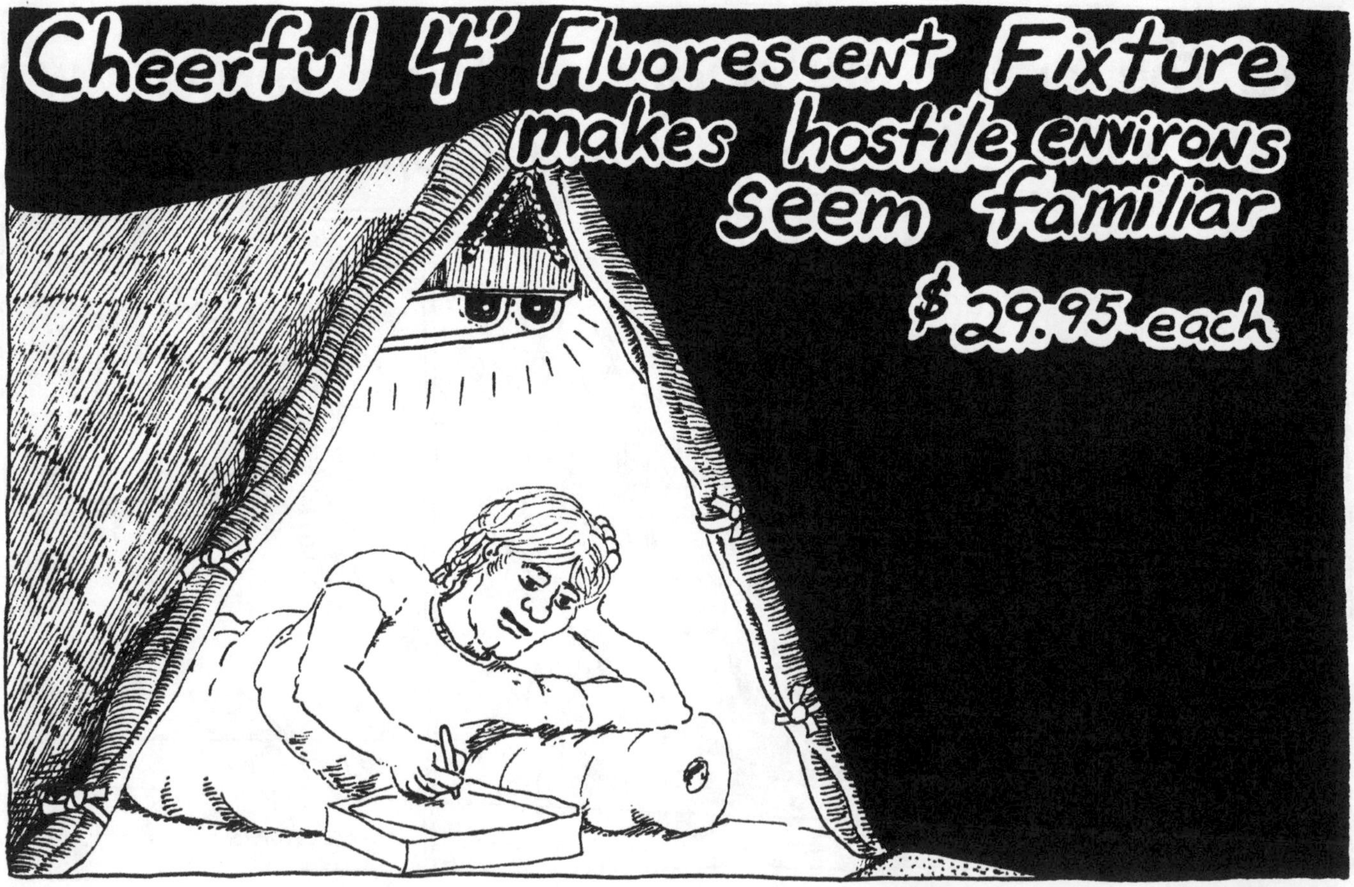
Cheerful 4' Fluorescent Fixture makes hostile environs seem familiar
$29.95 each

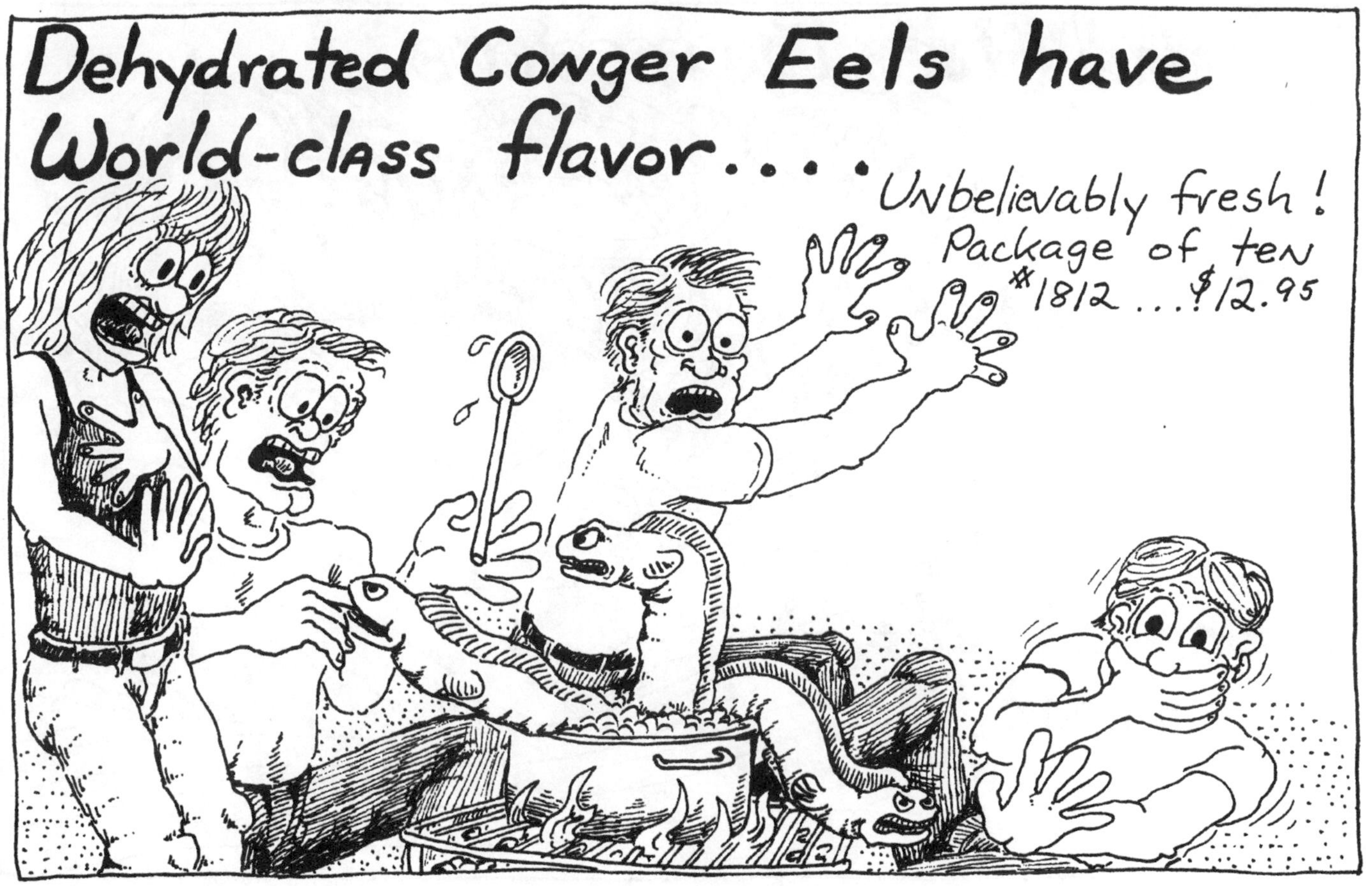

Dehydrated Conger Eels have World-class flavor....
Unbelievably fresh! Package of ten #1812 ...$12.95

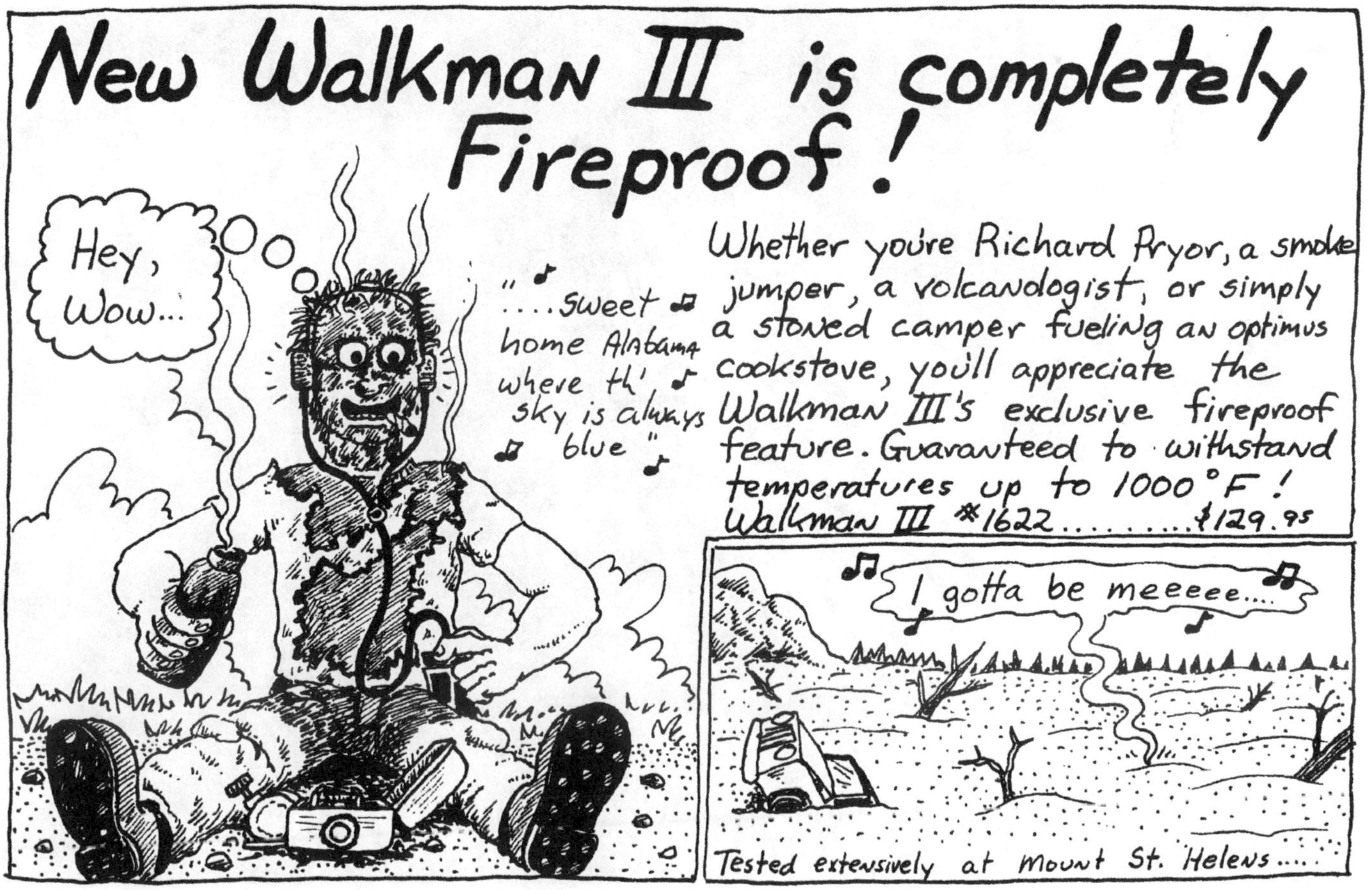

New Walkman III is completely Fireproof!
Hey, Wow...
"...Sweet home Alabama where th' sky is always blue"
Whether you're Richard Pryor, a smoke jumper, a volcanologist, or simply a stoned camper fueling an optimus cookstove, you'll appreciate the Walkman III's exclusive fireproof feature. Guaranteed to withstand temperatures up to 1000°F!
Walkman III #1622..........$129.95
I gotta be meeeee....
Tested extensively at Mount St. Helens....

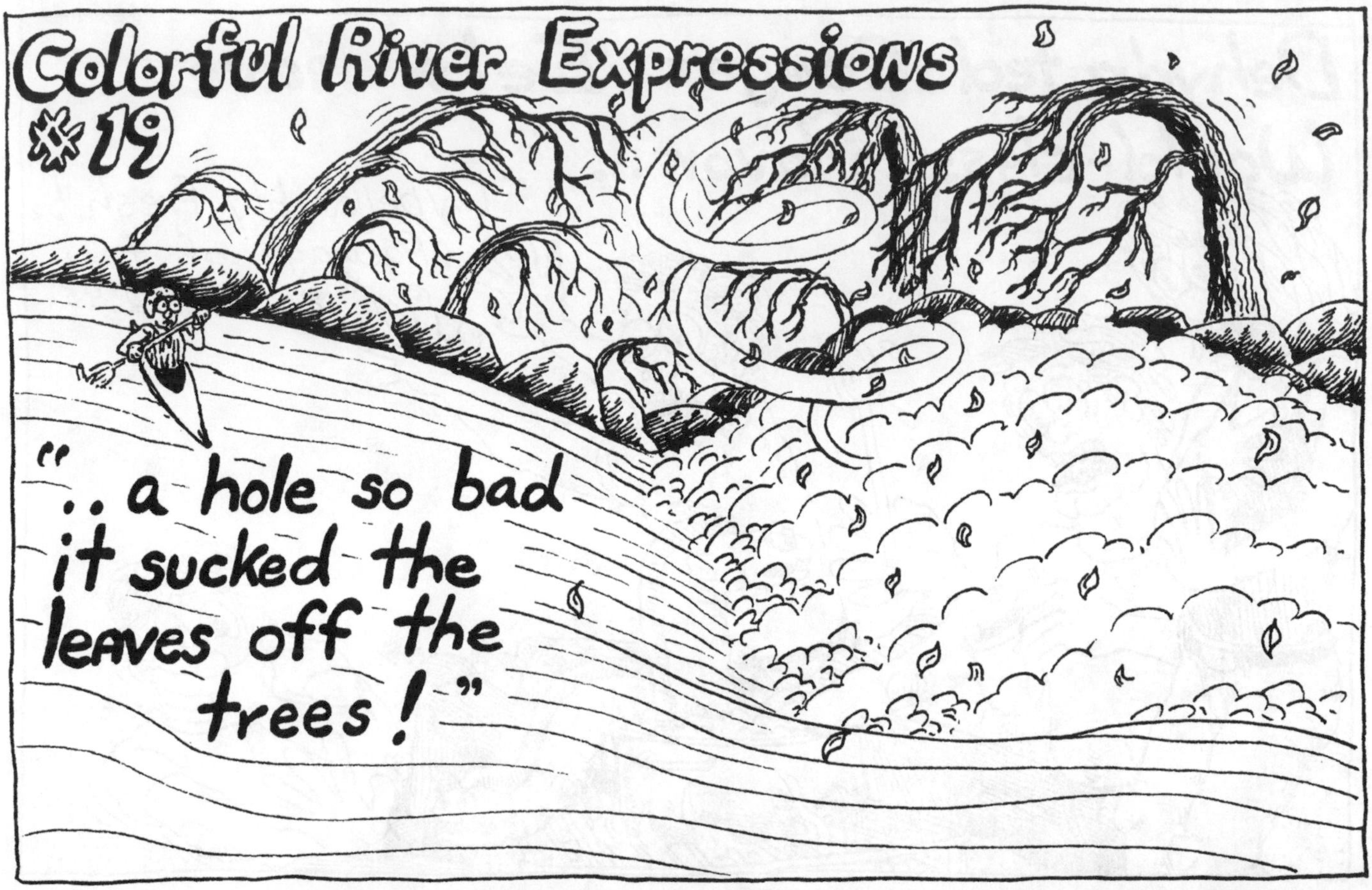
Colorful River Expressions #19
"..a hole so bad it sucked the leaves off the trees!"

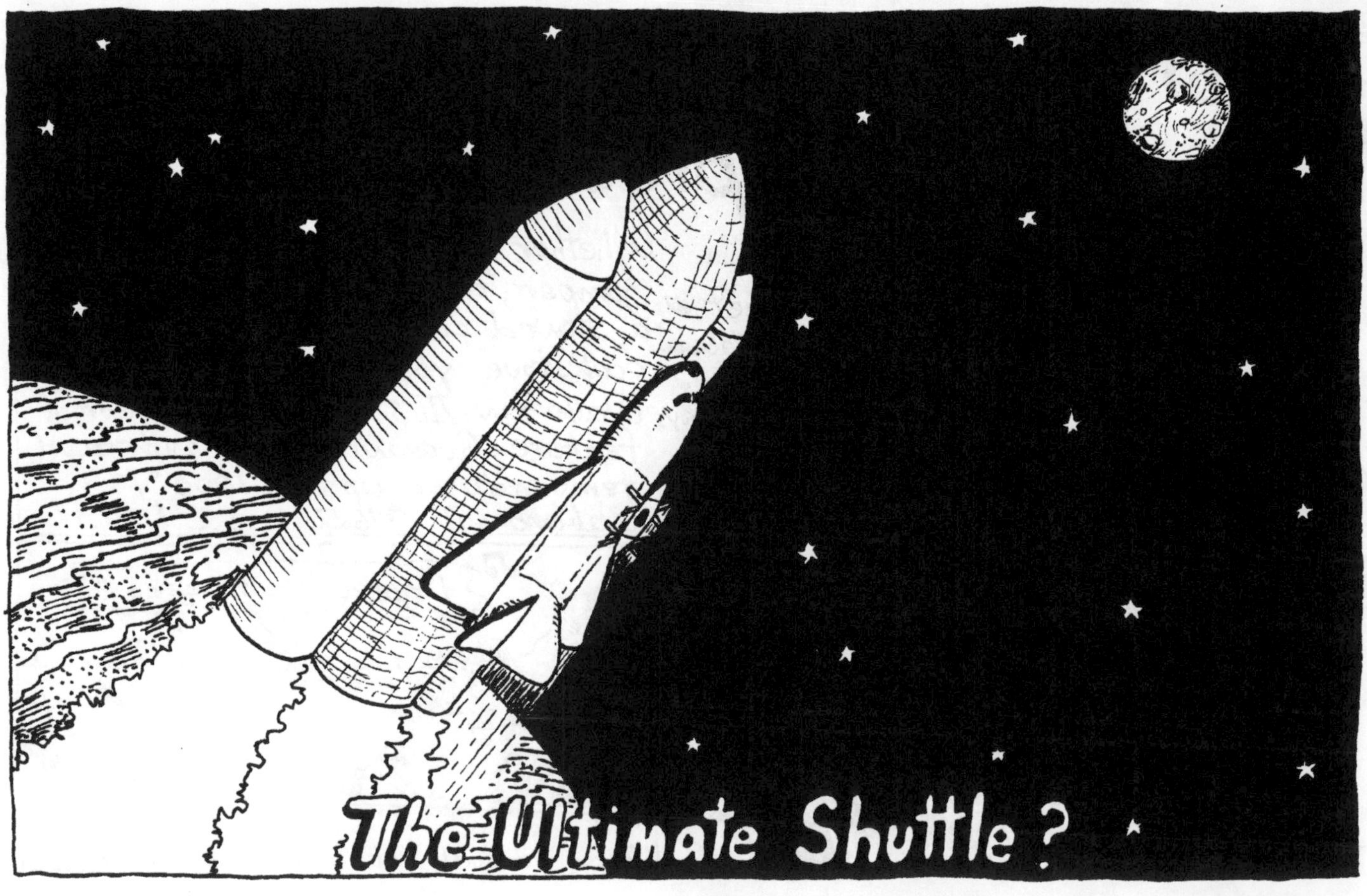
The Ultimate Shuttle?

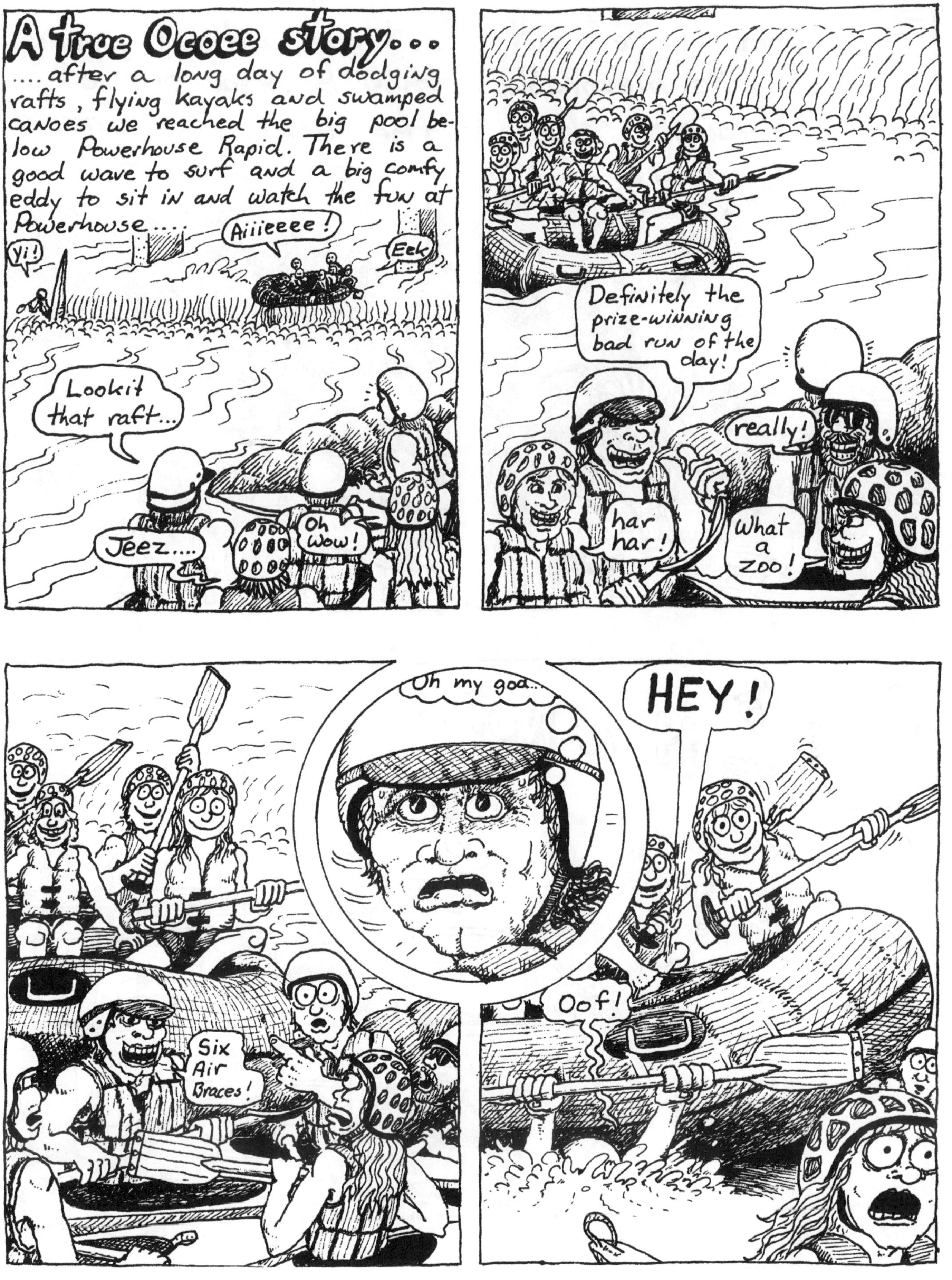
A true Ocoee story...
....after a long day of dodging rafts, flying kayaks and swamped canoes we reached the big pool below Powerhouse Rapid. There is a good wave to surf and a big comfy eddy to sit in and watch the fun at Powerhouse....
Yi!
Aiiieeee!
Eek
Lookit that raft...
Jeez....
Oh wow!
Definitely the prize-winning bad run of the day!
really!
har har!
What a zoo!
Oh my god...
HEY!
Six Air Braces!
Oof!

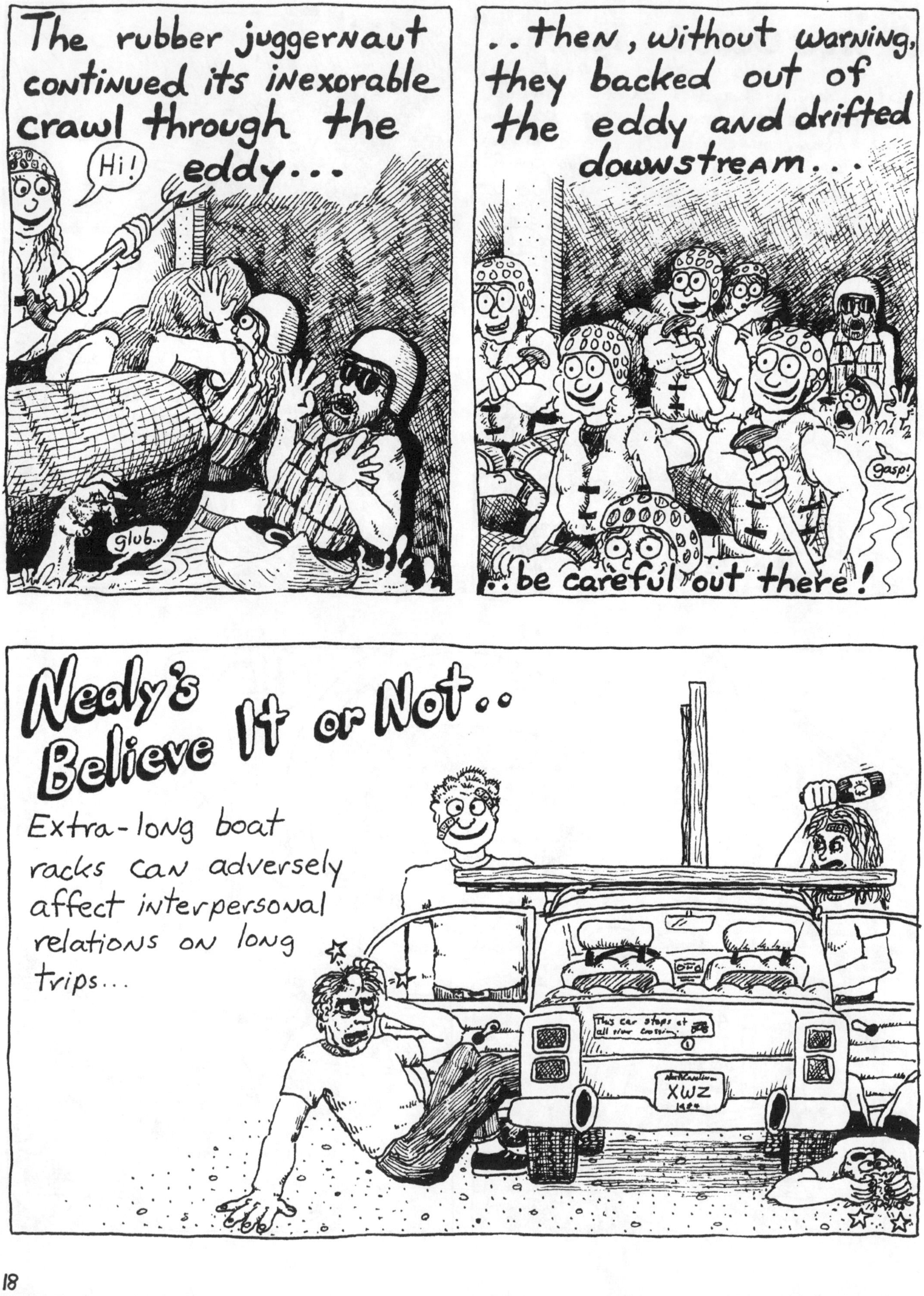
The rubber juggernaut continued its inexorable crawl through the eddy...
Hi!
glub...
..then, without warning, they backed out of the eddy and drifted downstream...
gasp!
..be careful out there!
Nealy's Believe It or Not..
Extra-long boat racks can adversely affect interpersonal relations on long trips...
XWZ

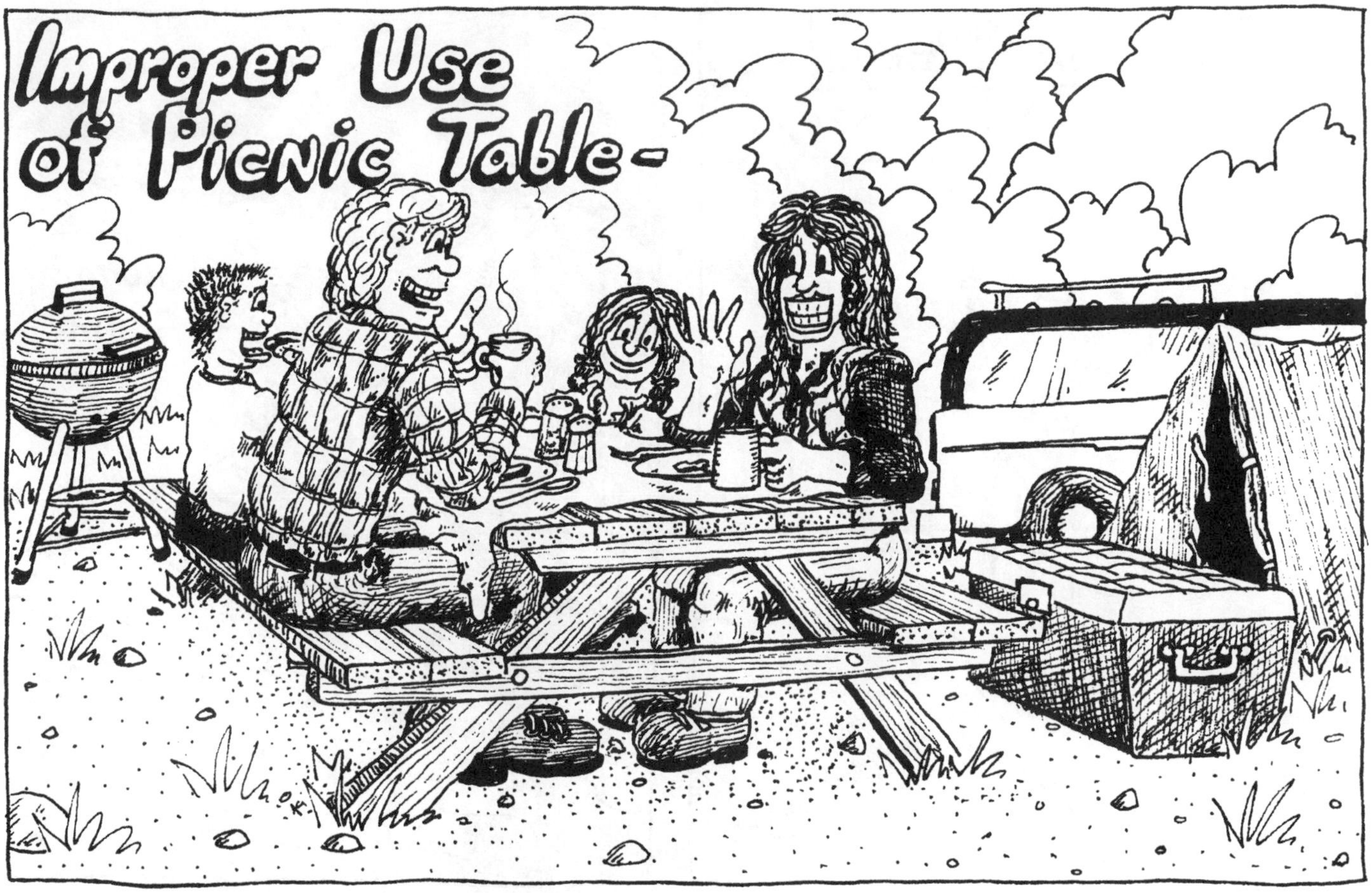
Improper Use of Picnic Table-

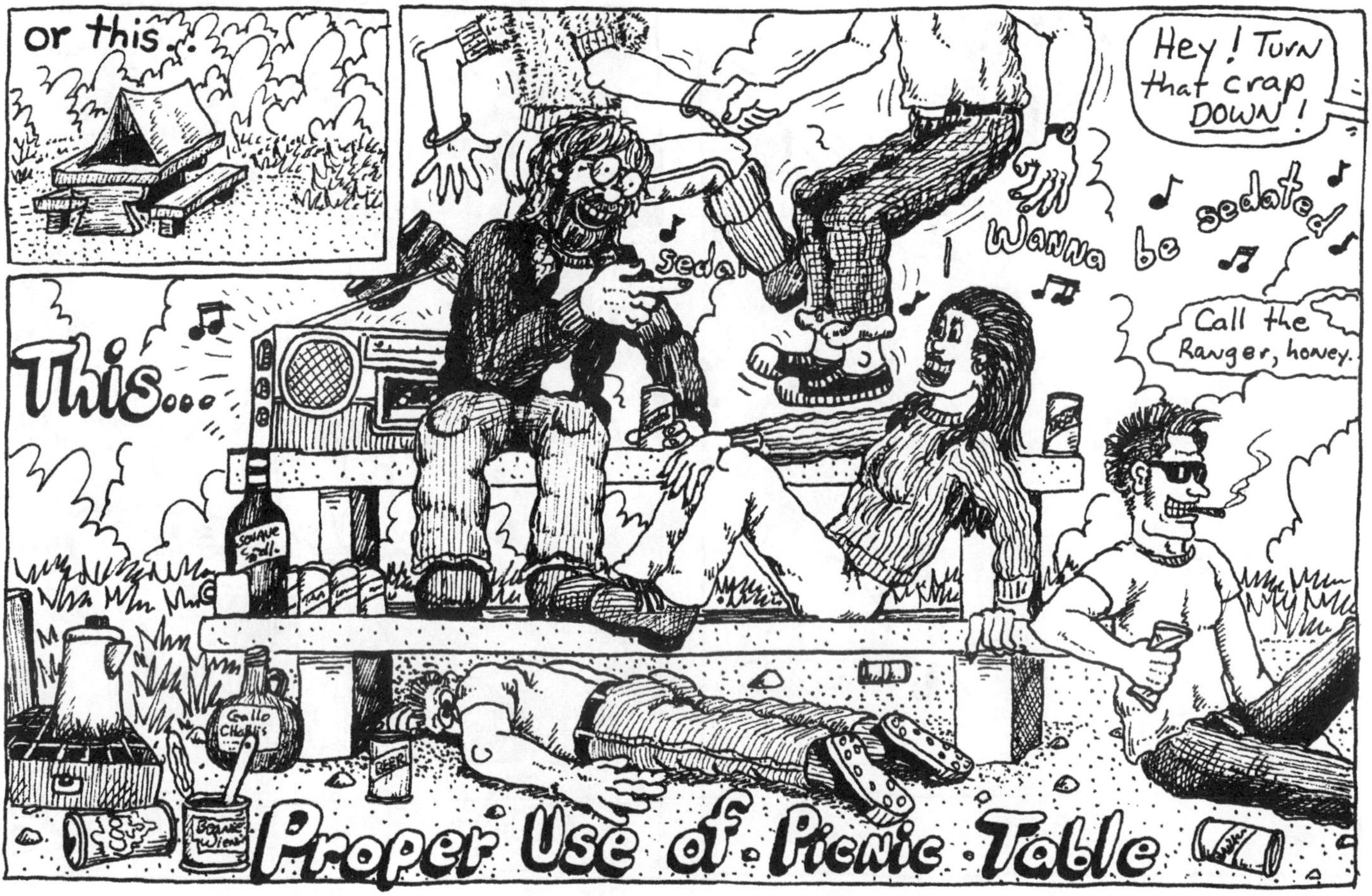
or this...
Hey! Turn that crap DOWN!
sedat
Wanna be sedated!
This...
Call the Ranger, honey.
Gallo Chablis
BEER
Proper Use of Picnic Table

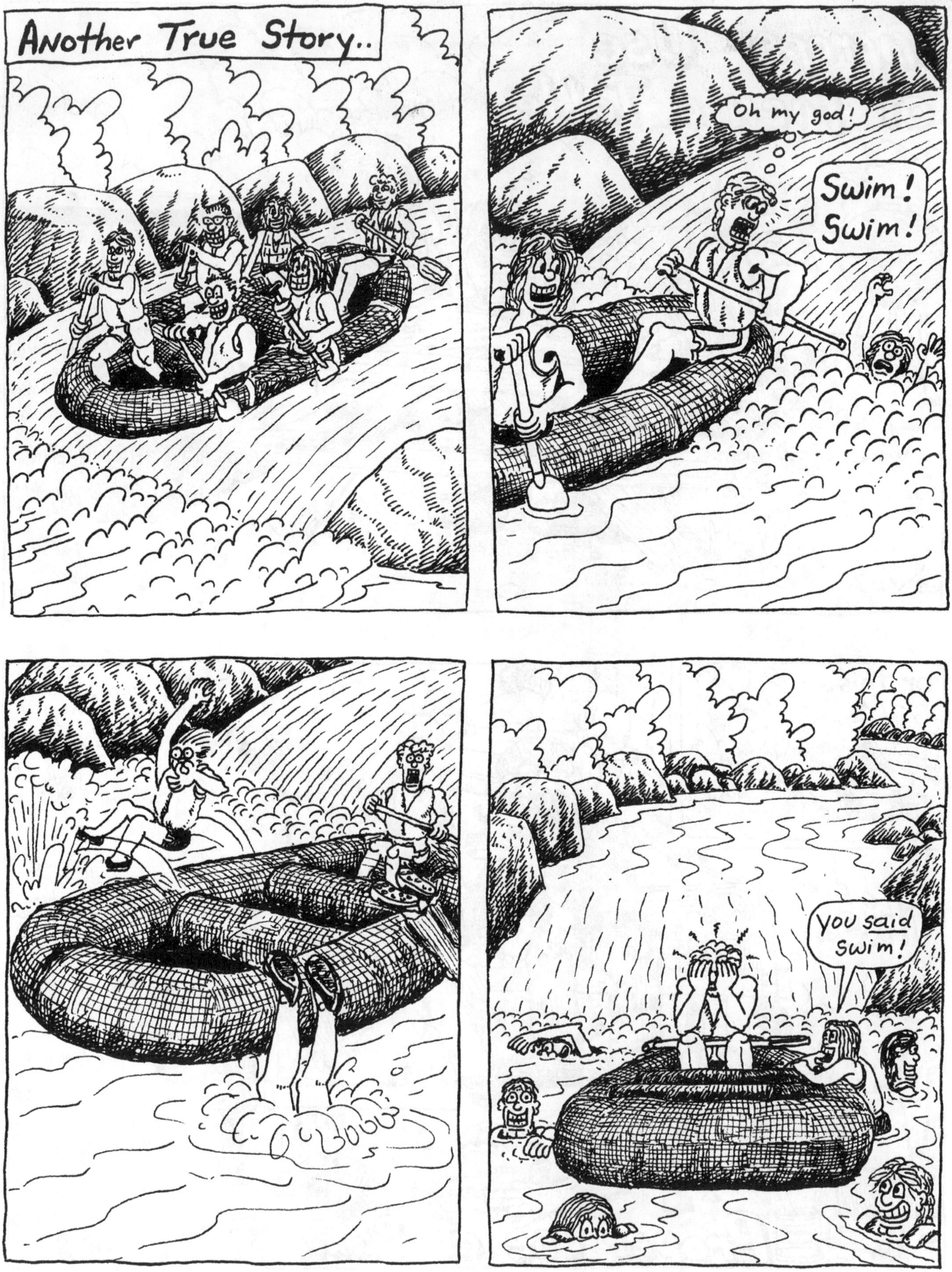
Another True Story..
Oh my god!
Swim! Swim!
you said swim!

Running Ice
Glacieryaking On The World's Mightiest Frozen River

Photographs of Epic Proportion

By

Vernon Krugerrand,

Mike Ultimate,

And

Rebus Teegrip

On the edge of the Abyss.. Vernon perches dangerously near the yawning bergschrund at the head of Baltoro Glacier......

A Gaggle of Visionaries

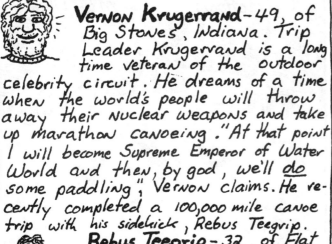

Vernon Krugerrand – 49, of Big Stones, Indiana. Trip Leader Krugerrand is a long time veteran of the outdoor celebrity circuit. He dreams of a time when the world's people will throw away their nuclear weapons and take up marathon canoeing. "At that point I will become Supreme Emperor of Water World and then, by god, we'll _do_ some paddling", Vernon claims. He recently completed a 100,000 mile canoe trip with his sidekick, Rebus Teegrip.

Rebus Teegrip – 32, of Flat Water, Ohio. Longtime friend and minion of Krugerrand, Rebus too wants to disarm the world and help Vernon rule the world community of boaters. "We could open up mandatory flatwater clinics worldwide and make some big

BIG bucks". His upcoming book on Glacier running technique will feature over 150 color photographs of the world's most formidable glaciers.

Mike Ultimate – 50, of Karma Bay, Florida. Team metaphysician and master glacieryak designer, Mike led the recent renaissance in solo canoe thwart design that has revolutionized the sport of canoe waltzing. Ultimate has been acclaimed as the Fodor Dostoyevsky of dynamic thwart design. "I was a little nervous when Vernon asked me to design the Glacieryak prototype", Ultimate admits, "When you're talking glaciers you're talking about forces far beyond anything found on any regular river. Glaciers carved the Great Lakes and made Indiana look like a golf course...think what one could do to a 16' glacieryak!"

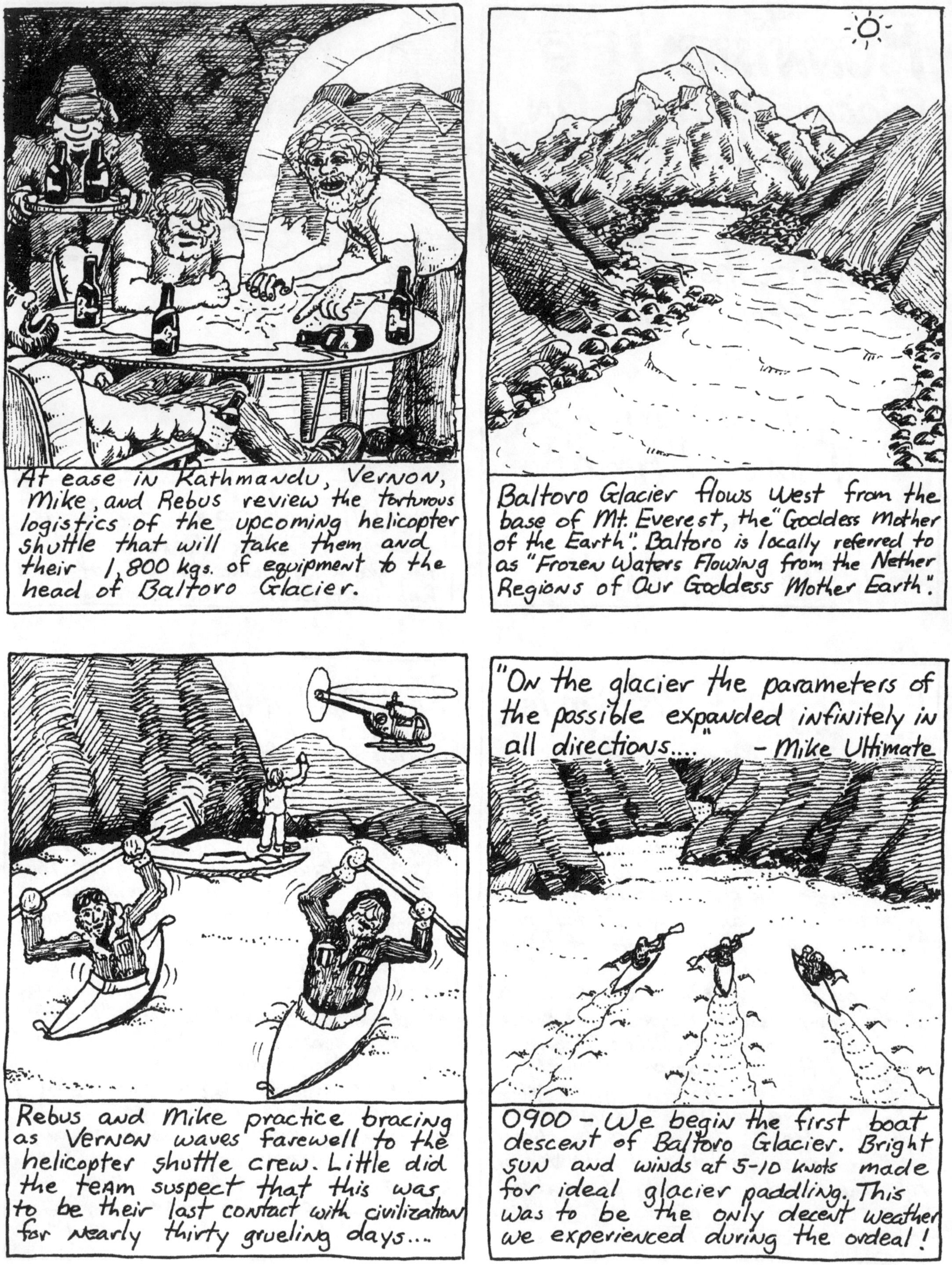
At ease in Kathmandu, VERNON, Mike, and Rebus review the torturous logistics of the upcoming helicopter shuttle that will take them and their 1,800 kgs. of equipment to the head of Baltoro Glacier.
Baltoro Glacier flows West from the base of Mt. Everest, the "Goddess Mother of the Earth". Baltoro is locally referred to as "Frozen Waters Flowing from the Nether Regions of Our Goddess Mother Earth".
Rebus and Mike practice bracing as VERNON waves farewell to the helicopter shuttle crew. Little did the team suspect that this was to be their last contact with civilization for nearly thirty grueling days...
"On the glacier the parameters of the possible expanded infinitely in all directions...." - Mike Ultimate
0900 - We begin the first boat descent of Baltoro Glacier. Bright SUN and winds at 5-10 knots made for ideal glacier paddling. This was to be the only decent weather we experienced during the ordeal!

"Our maximum top speed was a 'glacial' 10 meters per hour," Krugerrand confessed, "but at that pace you really develop a heightend awareness of the glacier."

Some beautiful ice formations....

Some other beautiful ice formations....

Day 3 – Mike suggests we practice our free-form glacieryak technique while ferrying to the opposite side of the glacier. This took two days. Rebus has begun to appear exhausted...

Day 5 – With a storm approaching, Vernon and Mike opt to push on while Rebus rests and brews up. They will rejoin 12 hours later, 150 meters down-glacier in the midst of a whiteout.

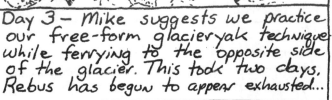

23

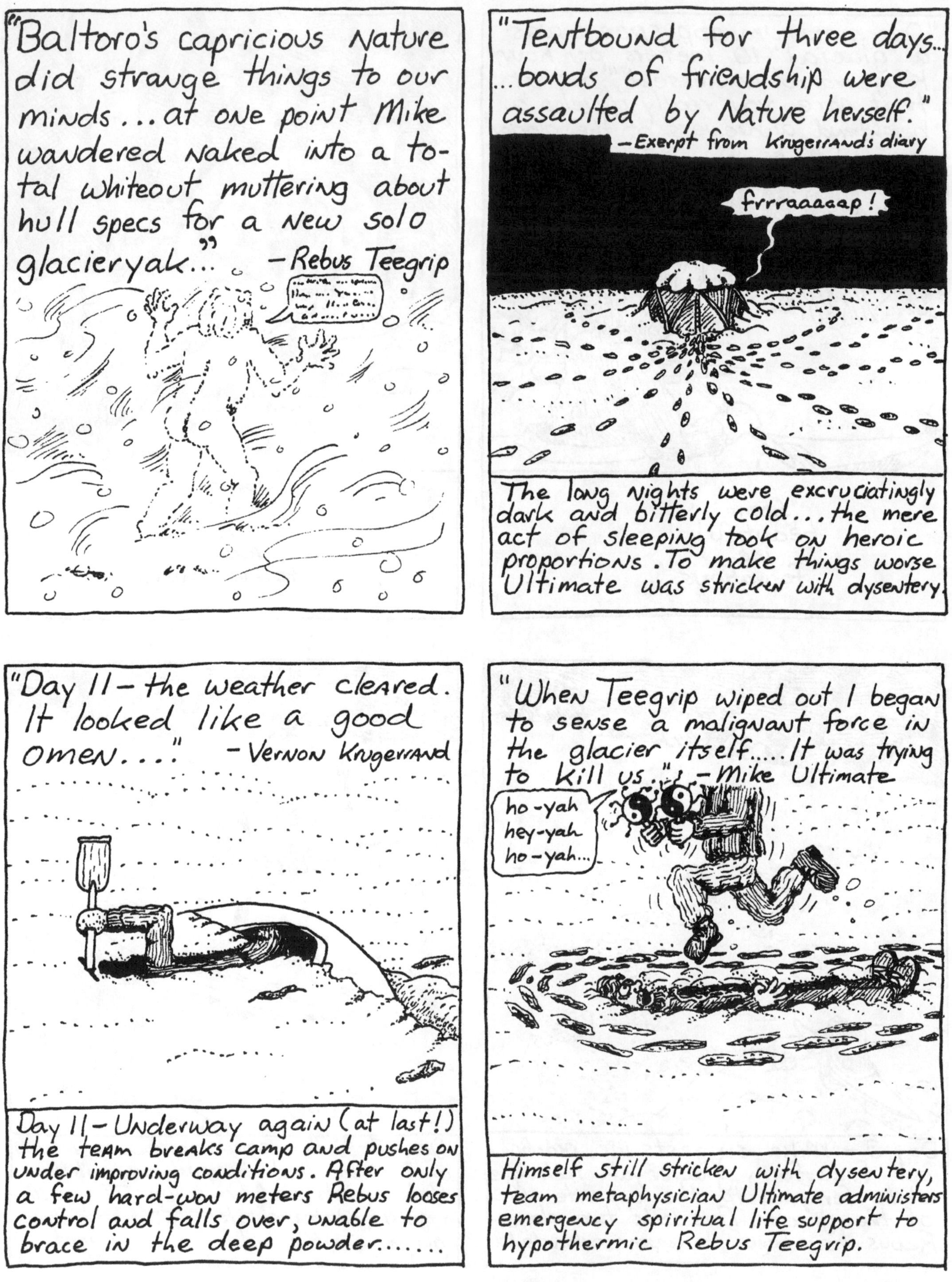

"Baltoro's capricious Nature did strange things to our minds...at one point Mike wandered naked into a total whiteout muttering about hull specs for a new solo glacieryak..." -Rebus Teegrip
"Tentbound for three days... ...bonds of friendship were assaulted by Nature herself." -Exerpt from Krugerrand's diary
frrraaaaap!
The long nights were excruciatingly dark and bitterly cold...the mere act of sleeping took on heroic proportions. To make things worse Ultimate was stricken with dysentery.
"Day 11-the weather cleared. It looked like a good omen..." -Vernon Krugerrand
Day 11-Underway again (at last!) the team breaks camp and pushes on under improving conditions. After only a few hard-won meters Rebus looses control and falls over, unable to brace in the deep powder......
"When Teegrip wiped out I began to sense a malignant force in the glacier itself.....It was trying to kill us..." -Mike Ultimate
ho-yah hey-yah ho-yah...
Himself still stricken with dysentery, team metaphysician Ultimate administers emergency spiritual life support to hypothermic Rebus Teegrip.

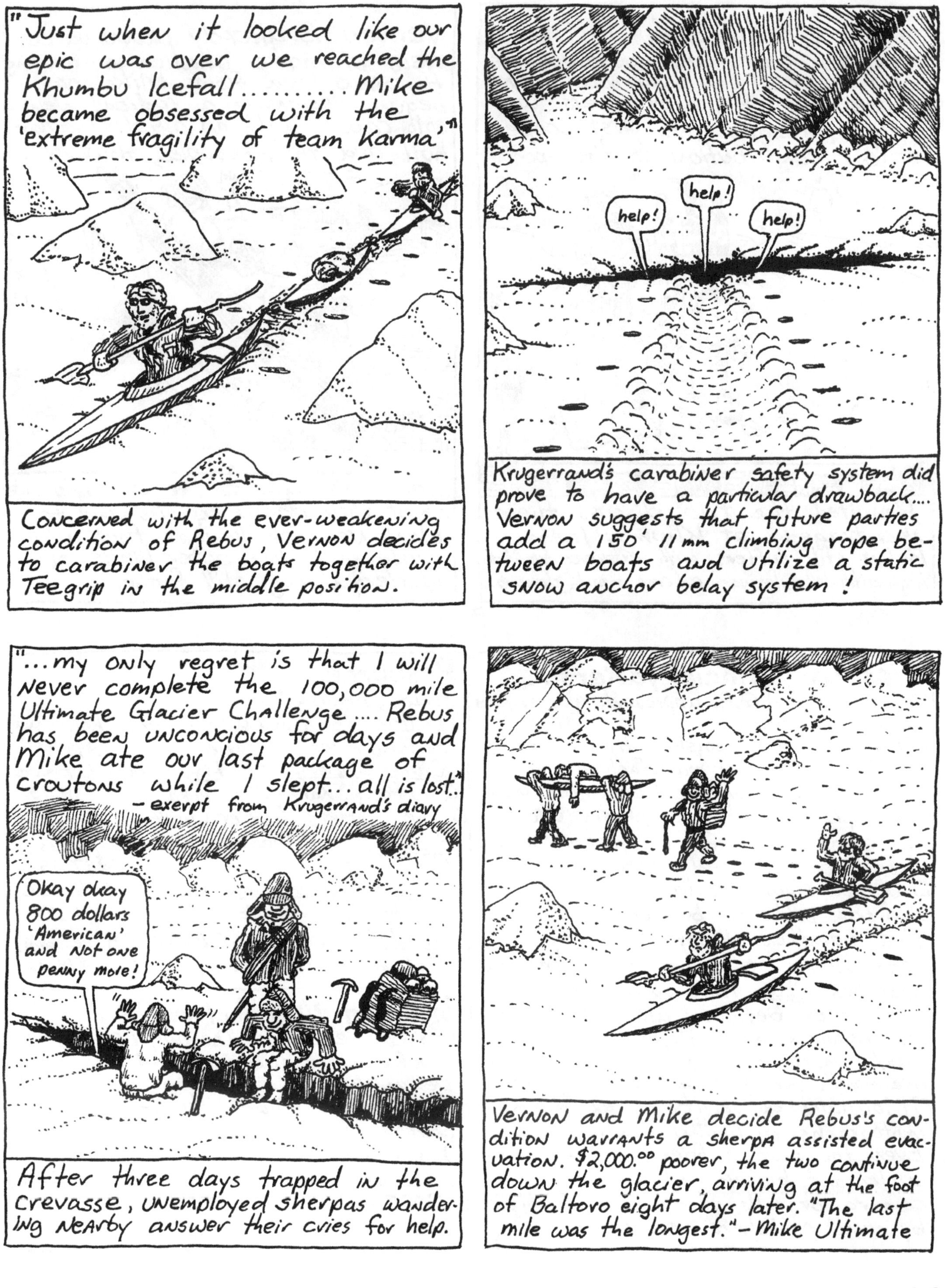
"Just when it looked like our epic was over we reached the Khumbu Icefall.........Mike became obsessed with the 'extreme fragility of team karma'"
Concerned with the ever-weakening condition of Rebus, Vernon decides to carabiner the boats together with Teegrip in the middle position.
help!
help!
help!
Krugerrand's carabiner safety system did prove to have a particular drawback.... Vernon suggests that future parties add a 150' 11mm climbing rope between boats and utilize a static snow anchor belay system!
"...my only regret is that I will never complete the 100,000 mile Ultimate Glacier Challenge .... Rebus has been unconcious for days and Mike ate our last package of croutons while I slept...all is lost."
- exerpt from Krugerrand's diary
Okay okay 800 dollars 'American' and not one penny more!
After three days trapped in the crevasse, unemployed sherpas wandering nearby answer their cries for help.
Vernon and Mike decide Rebus's condition warrants a sherpa assisted evacuation. $2,000.00 poorer, the two continue down the glacier, arriving at the foot of Baltovo eight days later. "The last mile was the longest." - Mike Ultimate

Back in Kathmandu Ultimate remarks, "Ours was an awesome achievment. I can only hope future generations of glacieryakers will fully appreciate the vast scope of our contribution to the sport."

Reunited the trio discuss their near-tragedy at Khumbu Icefall. Rebus still suffers with extensive frostbite, high altitude pulmonary edema, & mild dementia.

Vernon is already planning a new ultimate challenge - running Hawaiian lava flows. Mike has begun designing a radical new solo canoe with an asbestos/kevlar hull and thermocoupled thwarts...

...and it's back to the States to write about their daring exploits and to plan new challenges that will surely push the outer limits of glacieryaking still further!

Tips for Glacieryakers...

☐ Use only A.G.A. approved glacieryaks and accessories.

☐ Make sure sponsorships by magazines and/or equipment manufacturers entail no awkward contract encumberances that place undue emphasis upon style _or_ successful completion of the expeditions stated objectives.

☐ When signing contracts with magazine and book publishers be sure to clarify that marathon glacieryakists construe "continuous" to mean actual time on glaciers PLUS time spent off the glacier or between glaciers while on resupply or R.&R. missions. Resupply and/or R.&R. time should not exceed one month per three months per quarter.

☐ Maintain exclusivity on expedition photographs by written contract only. Even the best of friends can experience unpleasant lawsuits when custody of a camera or rolls of film are disputed by rival publishers or magazines.

Resources -
Books, information...

☐ _Baltoro the Hard Way_ - Vernon Krugerrand, Sea Snail Press, Ontario, 1983 ....$19.95

☐ _Games Glacieryakists Play_ - Mike Ultimate, Guru Press, Karma Bay, 1983 .... $18.95

☐ _The Ultimate Glacier Challenge_, _The True Story_ - Rebus Teegrip, Flatwater Press, New York, 1983............... $17.95

☐ _Solo on Baltoro_, _My Epic_ - M. Ultimate, Guru Press, Karma Bay, 1983...... $16.95

☐ _Medicine for Glacieryakers_ - R. Teegrip, Flatwater Press, New York, 1983...$15.95

Equipment Manufacturers -
Tao Glaciercraft - The only A.G.A. approved manufacturer of glacieryaks and accessories. Designed by Master Designer and Thwart Aesthetician Mike Ultimate. Tao Glaciercraft, Box 69, Karma Bay, Florida

Organizations -
American Glacieryak Association (A.G.A.)
P.O. Box 69
Karma Bay, Florida

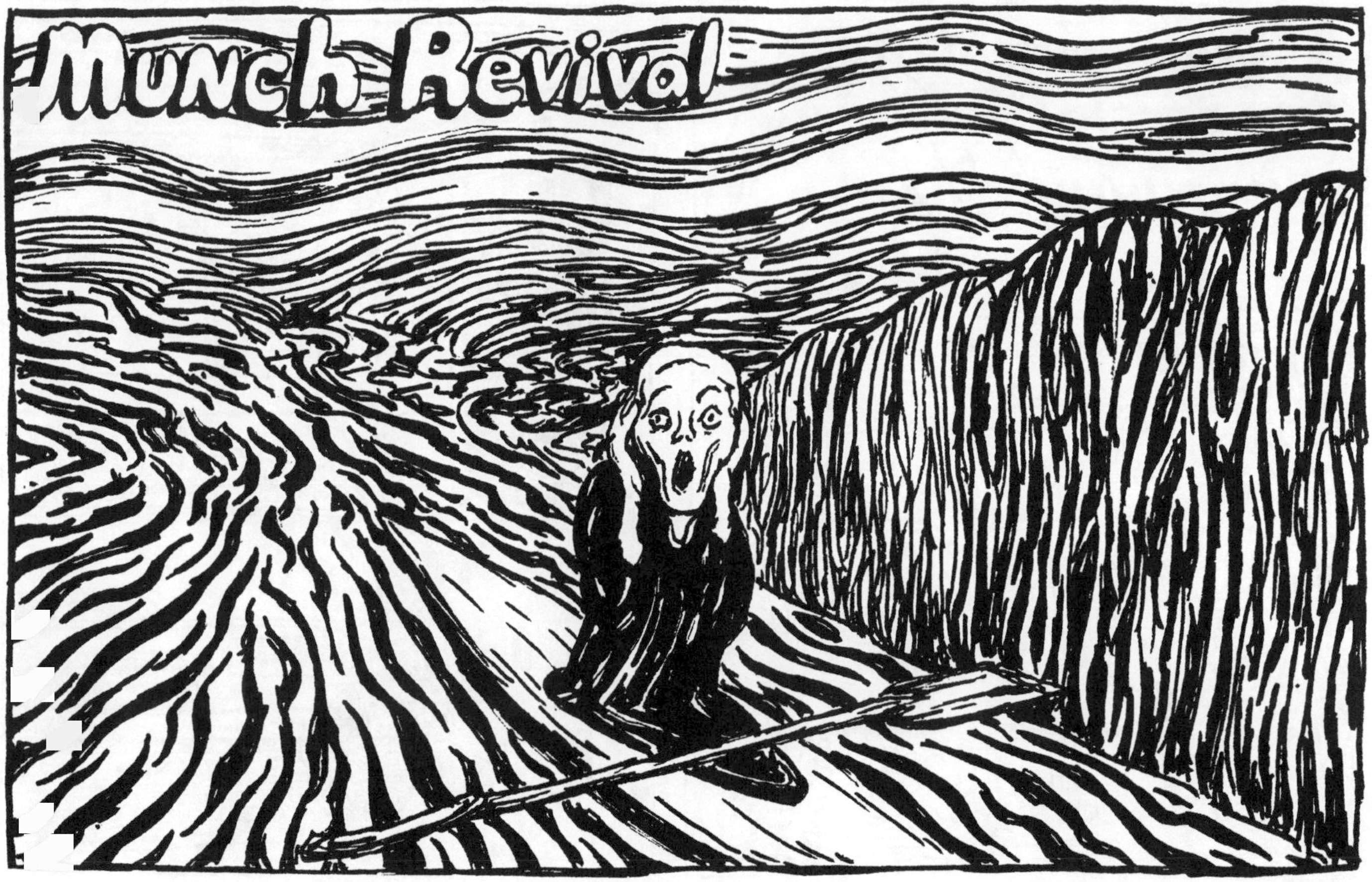
Munch Revival

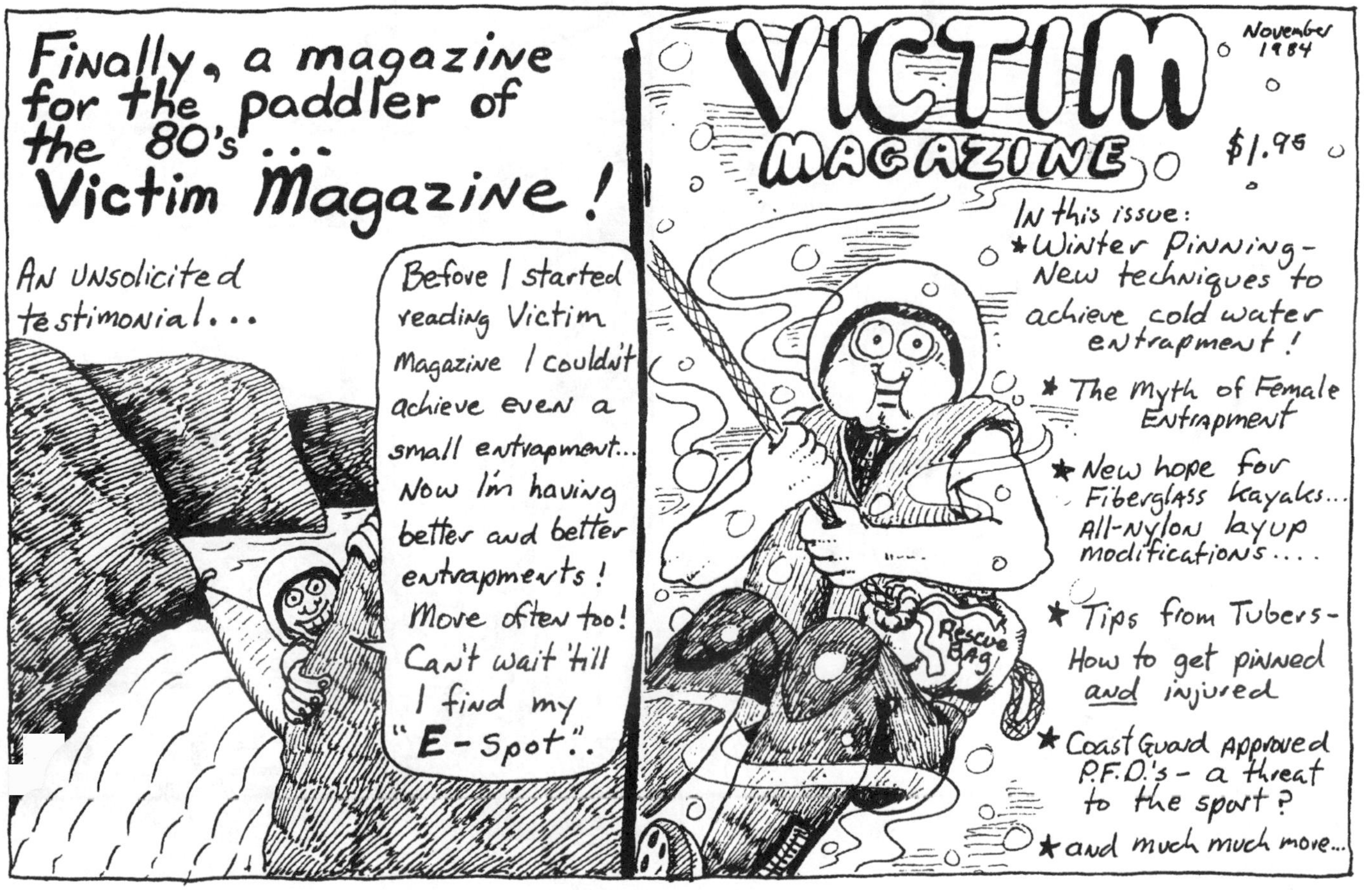
Finally, a magazine for the paddler of the 80's ... Victim Magazine!
An unsolicited testimonial...
Before I started reading Victim Magazine I couldn't achieve even a small entrapment... Now I'm having better and better entrapments! More often too! Can't wait 'till I find my "E-Spot".
VICTIM MAGAZINE
November 1984
$1.95
In this issue:
★Winter Pinning - New techniques to achieve cold water entrapment!
★The Myth of Female Entrapment
★New hope for Fiberglass kayaks... All-nylon layup modifications....
★Tips from Tubers - How to get pinned and injured
★Coast Guard Approved P.F.D.'s - a threat to the sport?
★and much much more...
Rescue Bag

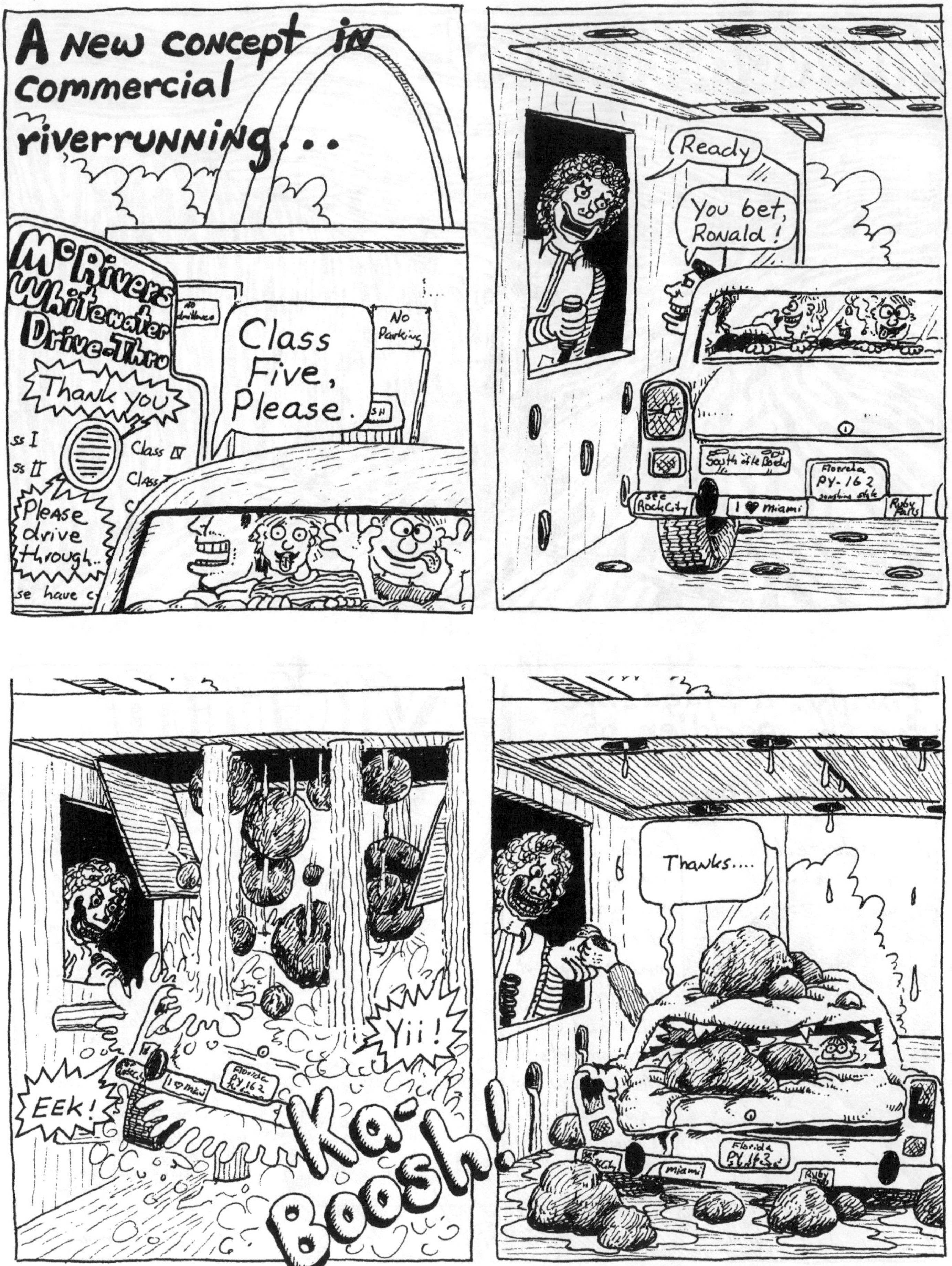

A new concept in commercial riverrunning...
McRivers Whitewater Drive-Thru
Thank you
Please drive through...
No Parking
Class Five, Please.
Ready
You bet, Ronald!
see Rock City
I ♥ miami
Florida PY-162
Ruby Falls
Yii!
EEK!
Ka-Boosh!
Thanks....

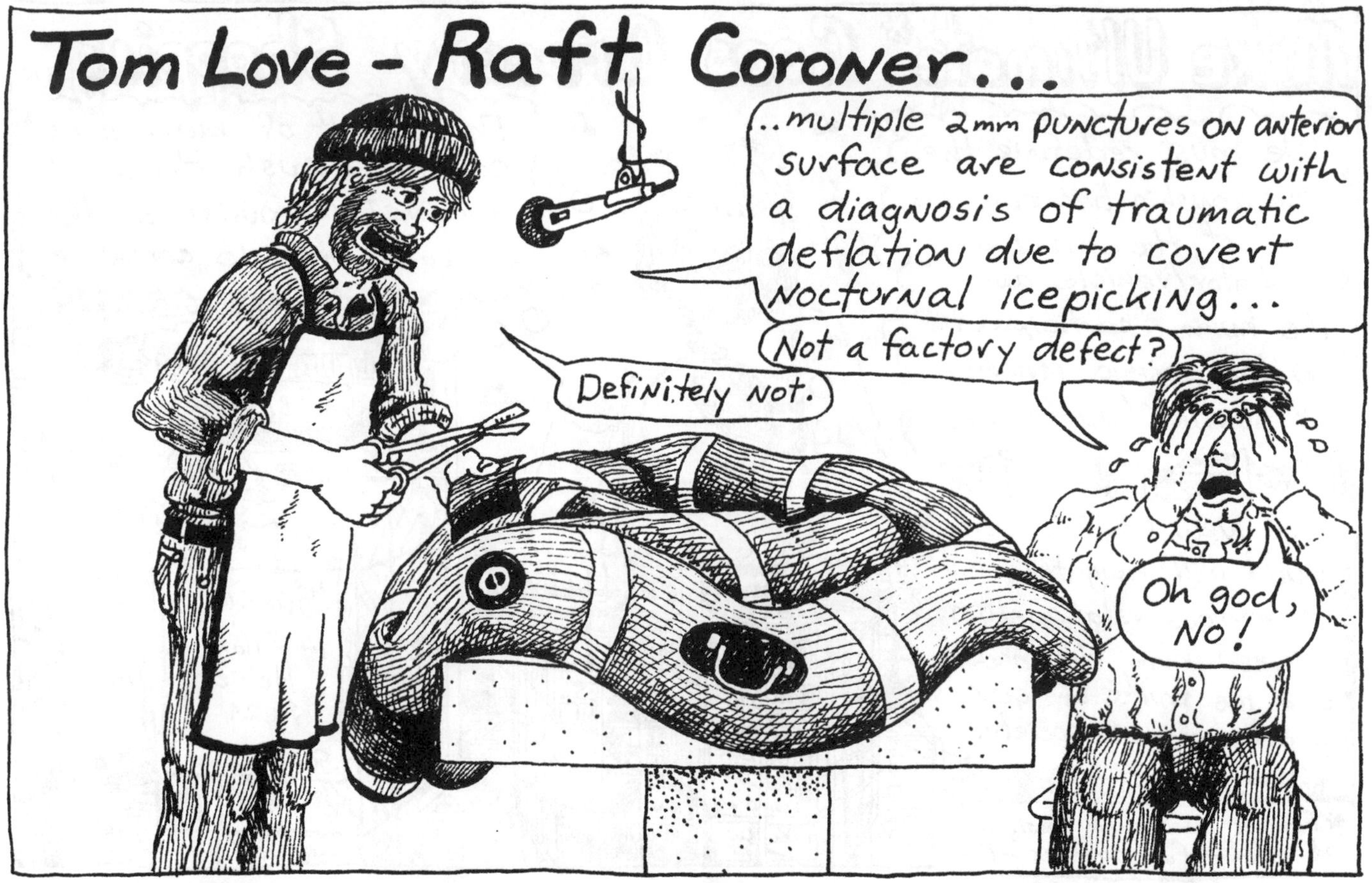
Tom Love - Raft Coroner...
..multiple 2mm punctures on anterior surface are consistent with a diagnosis of traumatic deflation due to covert nocturnal icepicking...
Not a factory defect?
Definitely not.
Oh god, No!

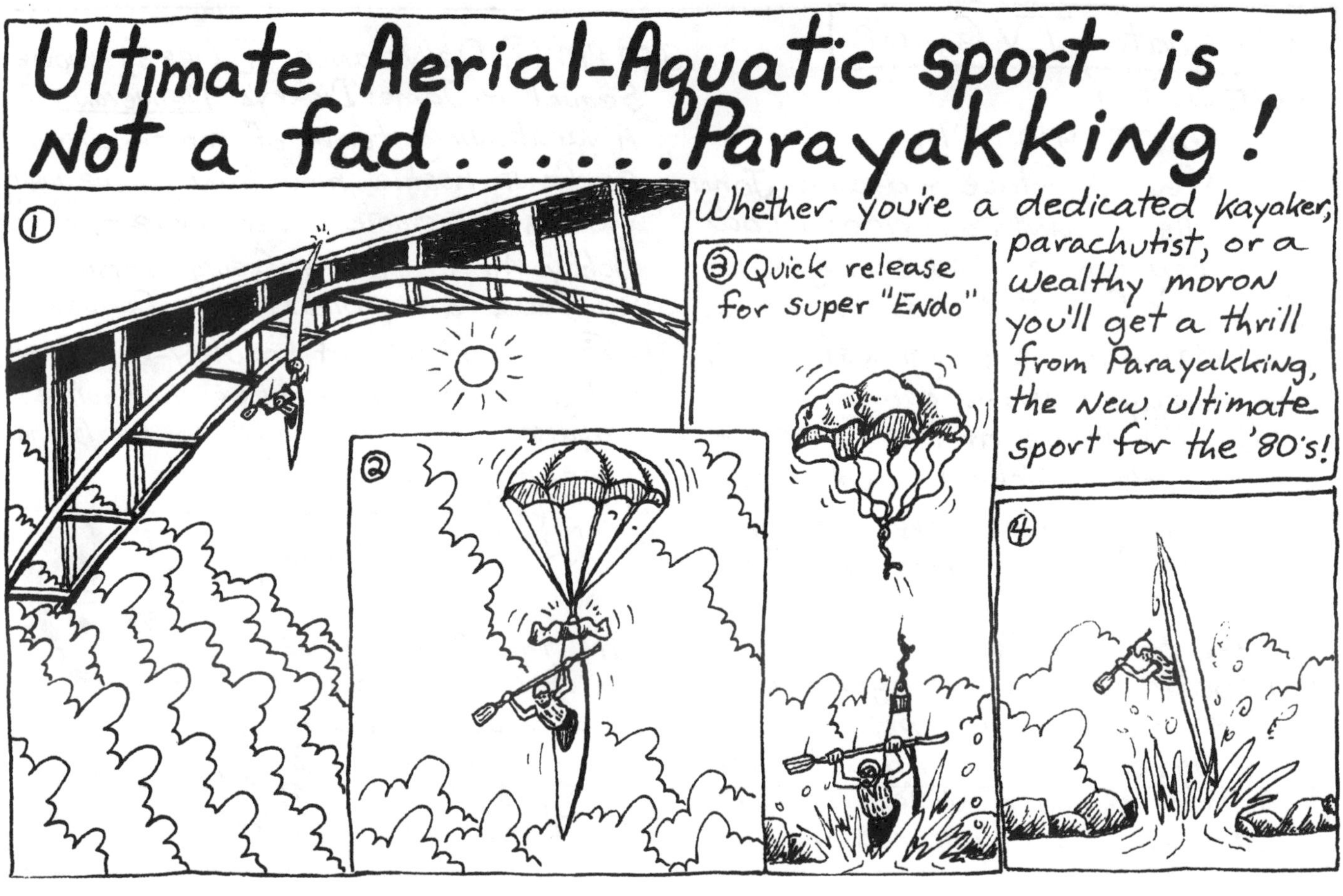
Ultimate Aerial-Aquatic sport is Not a fad......Parayakking!
①
Whether you're a dedicated kayaker, parachutist, or a wealthy moron you'll get a thrill from Parayakking, the new ultimate sport for the '80's!
②
③ Quick release for super "Endo"
④

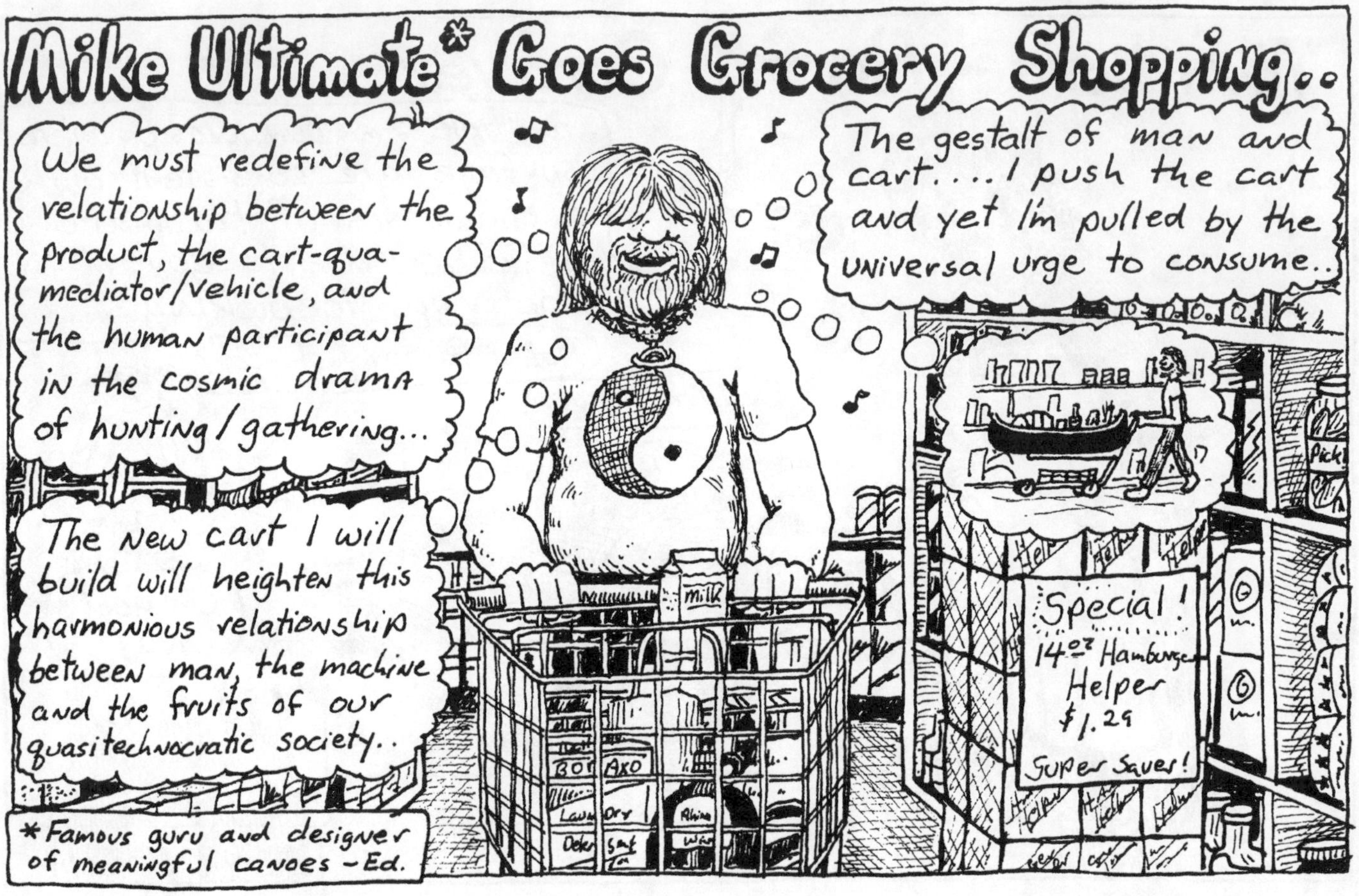
Mike Ultimate* Goes Grocery Shopping..
We must redefine the relationship between the product, the cart-qua-mediator/vehicle, and the human participant in the cosmic drama of hunting/gathering...
The gestalt of man and cart..../ push the cart and yet I'm pulled by the universal urge to consume..
The new cart I will build will heighten this harmonious relationship between man, the machine and the fruits of our quasitechnocratic society..
Special! 14oz Hamburger Helper $1.29 Super Saver!
milk
*Famous guru and designer of meaningful canoes -Ed.

Whitewater TV Guide

TUESDAY

4:30 PM To 9:00 P.M.

7:30 ⑤ Peyson's Place - drama - John Boy sells an anthrax-ridden cow so he can buy a new racing K-1.

⑦ People's Court - Cases involve a civil damage suit against T.V.A. and a kayak manufacturer.

⑪ ② Little House at the Takeout - drama - Pa (Michael Landon) takes a church group down the river and discovers Preacher Jim-Bob (John Ritter) is in reality Rev. Jim Jones of the People's Temple....

㊽ Boating for Dollars - game show - Expert kayakers compete for trips and prizes by running a kayak simulator down a video river - the HBO-Bio. Host: Lee Majors

8:00 PM ⑦ Deliverance II (1983) - movie - Sequel to James Dickey's Deliverance - A vacationing team of mercenaries confront hostile mountain people while rafting a remote river gorge - Bobby: Mr. T, Lewis - George Peppard, Ed - Jamie Farr, Drew - John Denver

② ⑤ The Dukes of Gauley - A reformed call girl borrows General Lee to shuttle kayakers who turn out to be Bolivian cocaine smugglers. Repeat.

Tonite

Deliverance II

The Sequel

It's the A-Team vs. the Beverly Hillbillies on a deadly river of death!?

8:00

Don't Miss It!

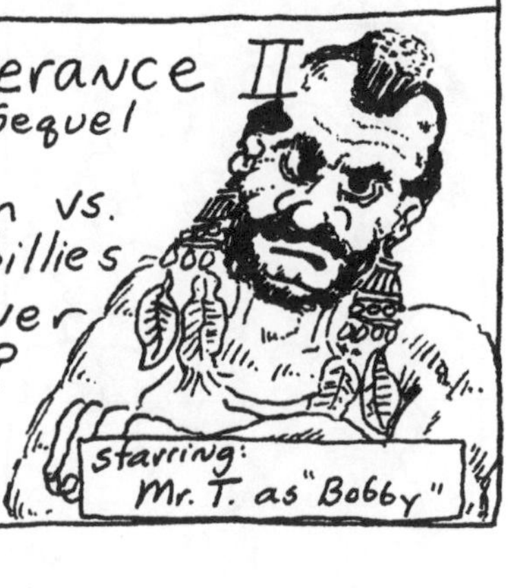
starring: Mr. T. as "Bobby"

Bo-John Schneider, Luke-Tom Wombat, Daisy-Barbara Bach

(22) Rep Talk - talk show - Tonight's guest sales reps discuss buying trends in the plastic kayak market. Host-Tom Schlinkert (repeat)

(HBO) Tuesday Night Hacky Sack Playoffs - sports - Live from Chili Bar on the American River in California, The Denver DooDahs and the Seattle Sopors compete for Natl. Championship.

(11) Lava! - drama - J.R. tricks Sue Ellen into running an overloaded beer raft too far left in Lava Falls. Sue Ellen has a nasty swim. J.R.-Larry Hagman, Sue Ellen-Linda Gray, Pam-Victoria Principal

(PBS) Nova - science documentary - "Two-bladed Scientists" - Kayaking biologists search for endangered species in the Tuolome River.

8:30 (22) Whitewater Week in Review - New - A synopsis of river-related News items from the past week - Hosts - James Brolin, Barbara Bach

(2) Magnum K-I - Magnum (Tom Selleck) becomes involved with a gangster-moll enrolled in his kayak clinic. Co-starring Dolly Parton

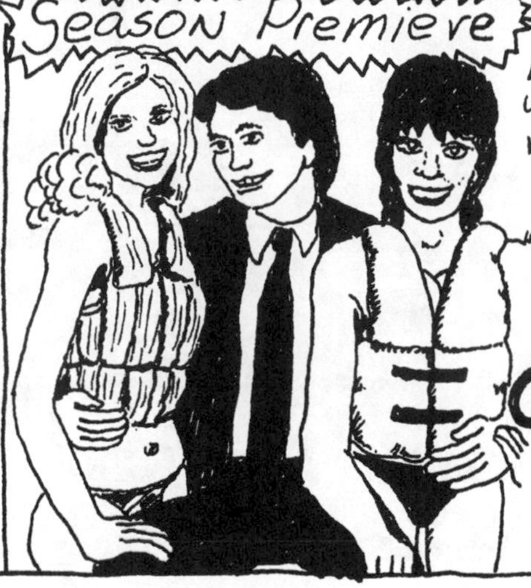
Season Premiere

Is this any way to run a raft company?

THREE'S RAFT COMPANY 12 WTCT

9:00 P.M. to 10:30 P.M.

9:00 (2) Survival of the Fittest - sports special - Famous climbers and kayakers dress up in suits and attempt to operate office machinery for big prizes. Host- Howard Cosell

(22) S.M.A.S.H. - drama - Hawkeye and Trapper John meet a group of vacationing Swedish stewardesses who have lost their raft guide and are stranded in the Grand Canyon. It's loads of laughs for the "raftin' 4077th". Special Guest Star - Veronica Hamel as "Olga".

(PBS) The Iowa Paddling Repertory Company performs flatwater canoe ballet under the direction of conductor/composer Mike Ultimate

(11) Slow and Dirty - Game show - Celebrity Bad Guys compete on a whitewater slalom course for money & prizes. Guests - Mr. T, Larry Hagman, Bruce Dern, Robert Mitchum.

(7) The Love Raft - comedy - On tonite's episode the crew of the Love Raft take a champagne cruise in the Grand Canyon of the Stikine River in British Columbia.

The Hole Warrior - Mel Gibson plays a disgruntled kayaker who is fed up with boorish paddlers in his favorite surfing hole.

Tonite! 10:00 PM WBCT

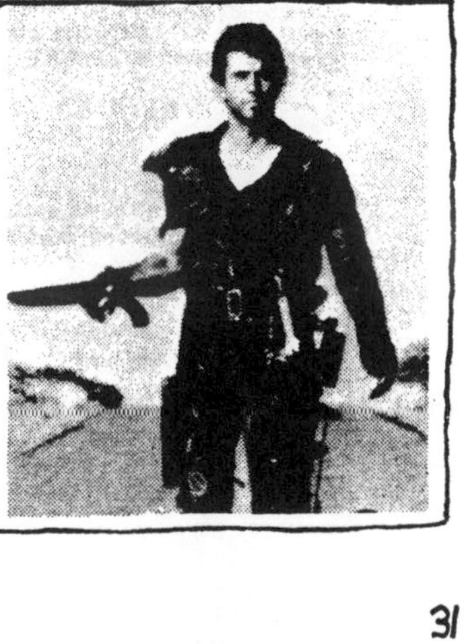

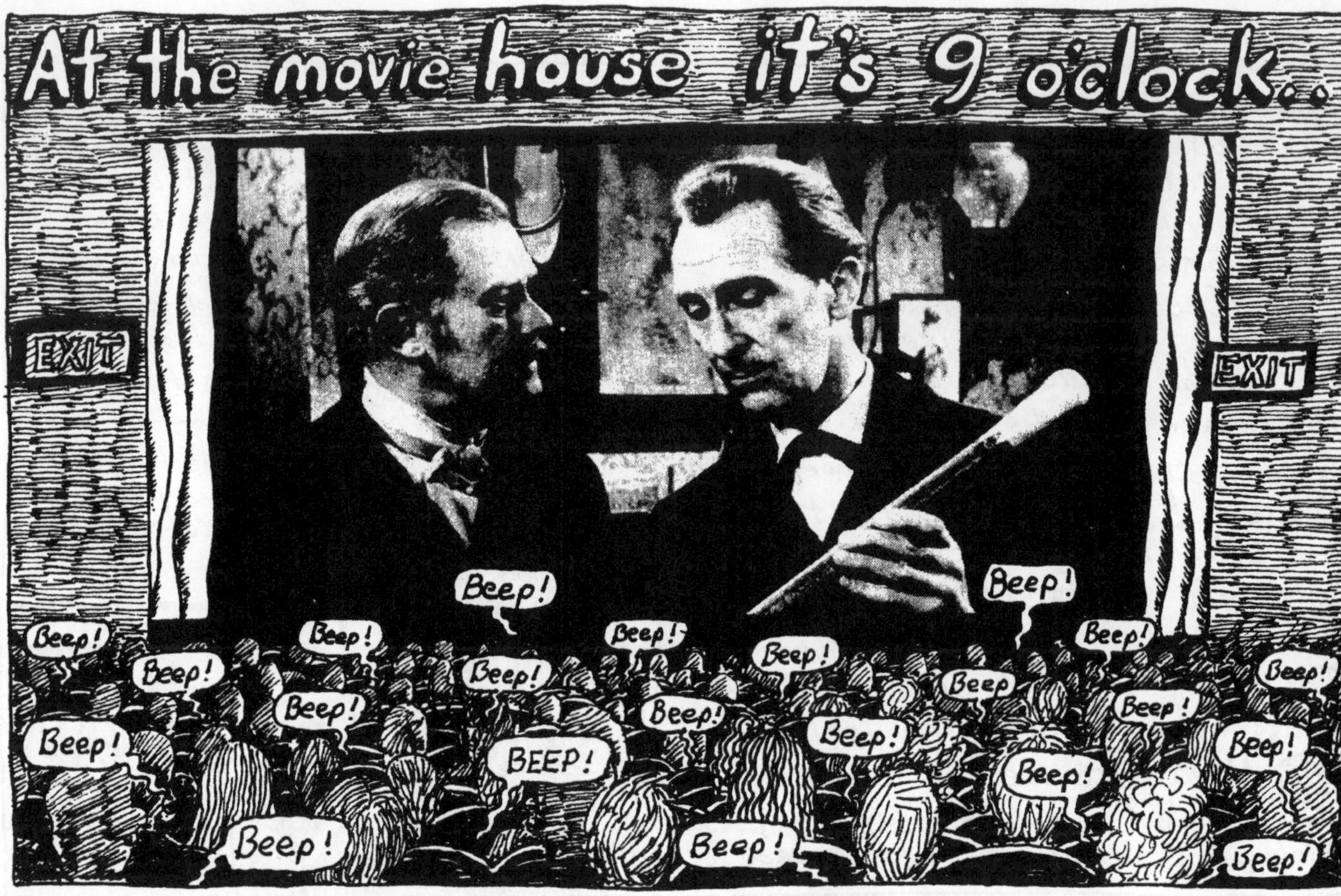
At the movie house it's 9 o'clock..
EXIT
EXIT
Beep!
Beep!
Beep!
Beep!
Beep!
Beep!
Beep!
Beep!
Beep!
Beep!
Beep!
Beep!
Beep!
Beep!
BEEP!
Beep!
Beep!
Beep!
Beep!
Beep!
Beep!
Beep!

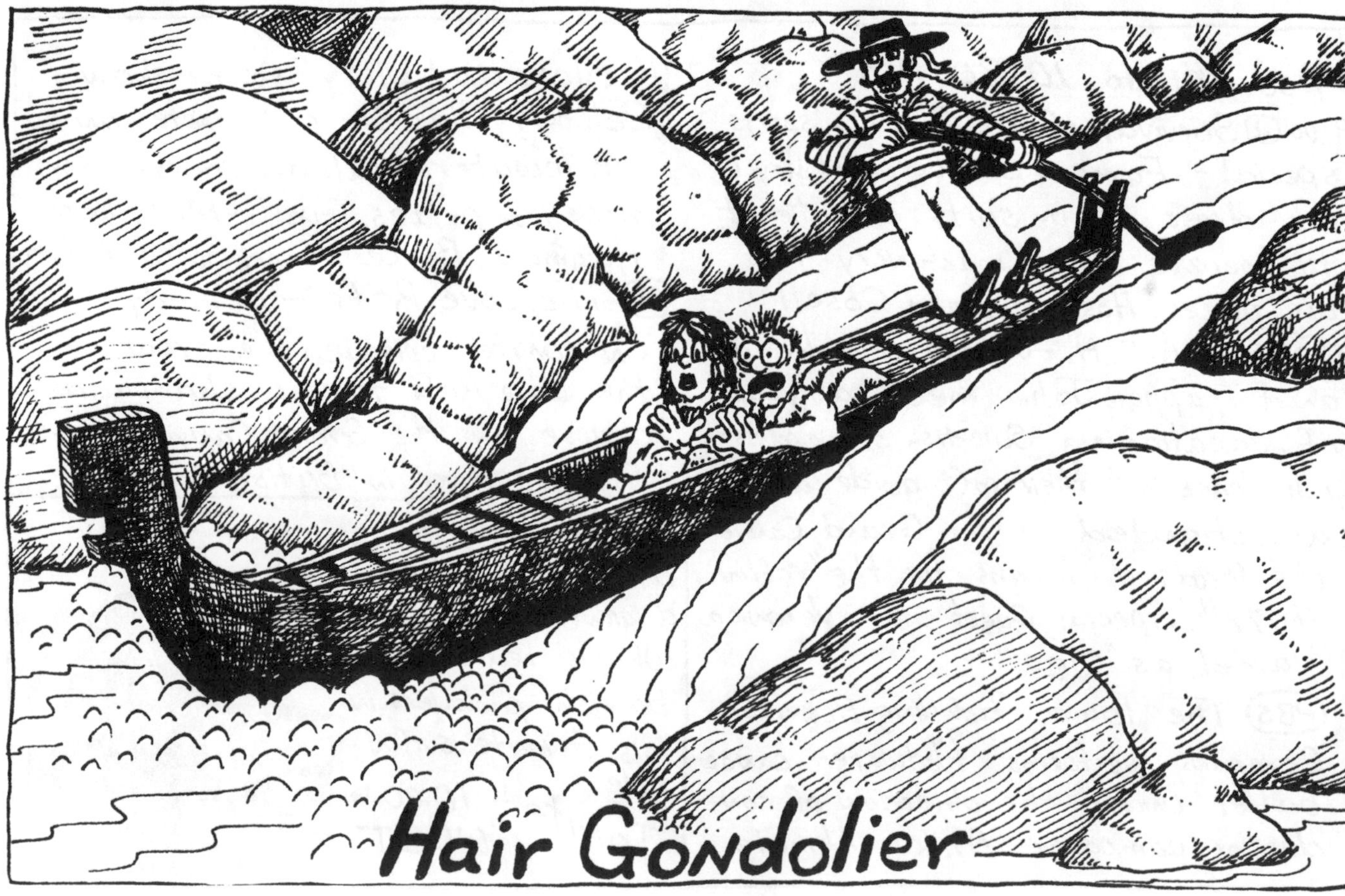
Hair Gondolier

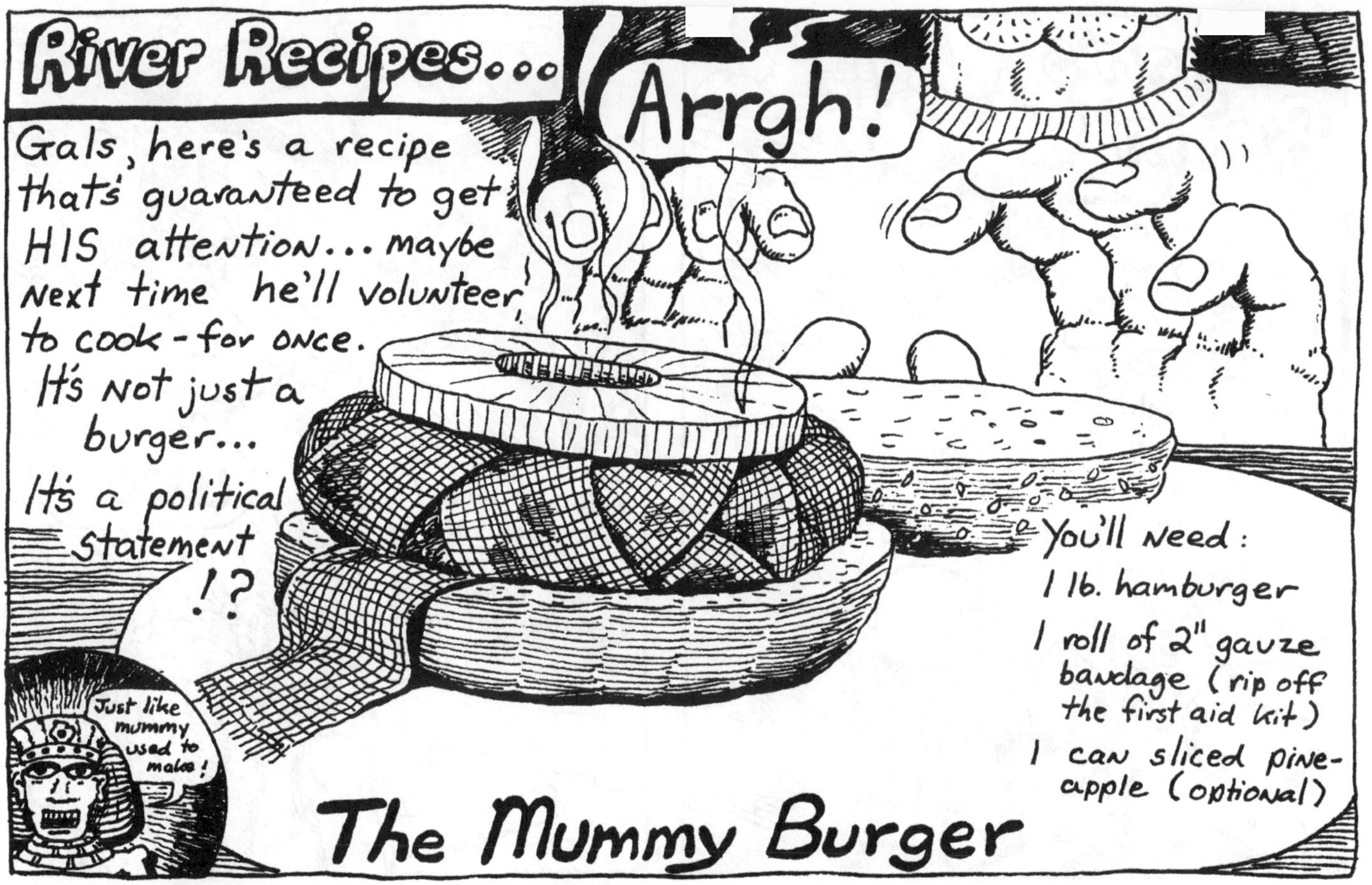
River Recipes...
Arrgh!
Gals, here's a recipe that's guaranteed to get HIS attention... maybe Next time he'll volunteer to cook - for once.
It's Not just a burger...
It's a political statement !?
Just like mummy used to make!
You'll Need:
1 lb. hamburger
1 roll of 2" gauze bandage (rip off the first aid kit)
1 can sliced pineapple (optional)
The Mummy Burger

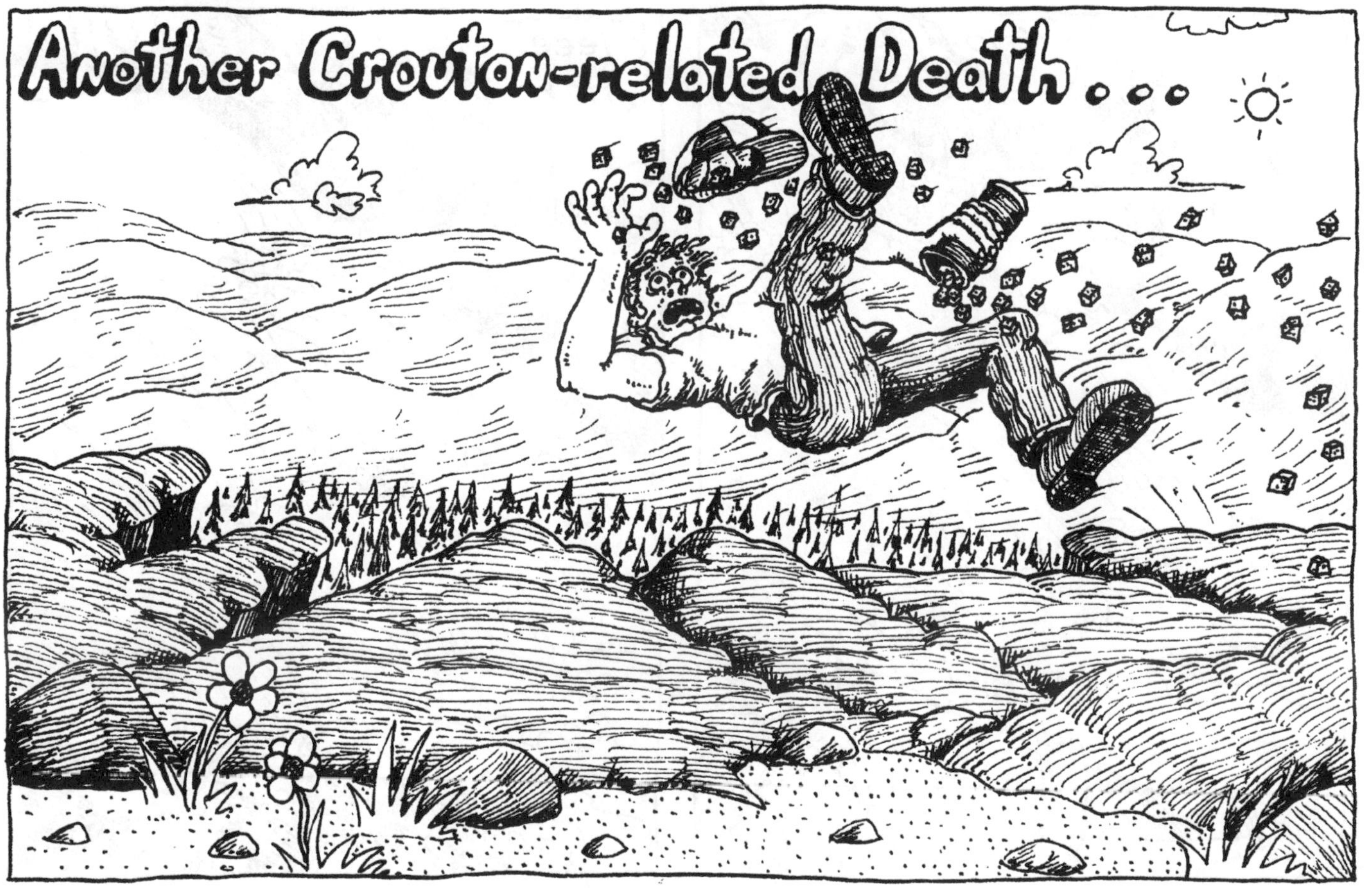
Another Crouton-related Death...

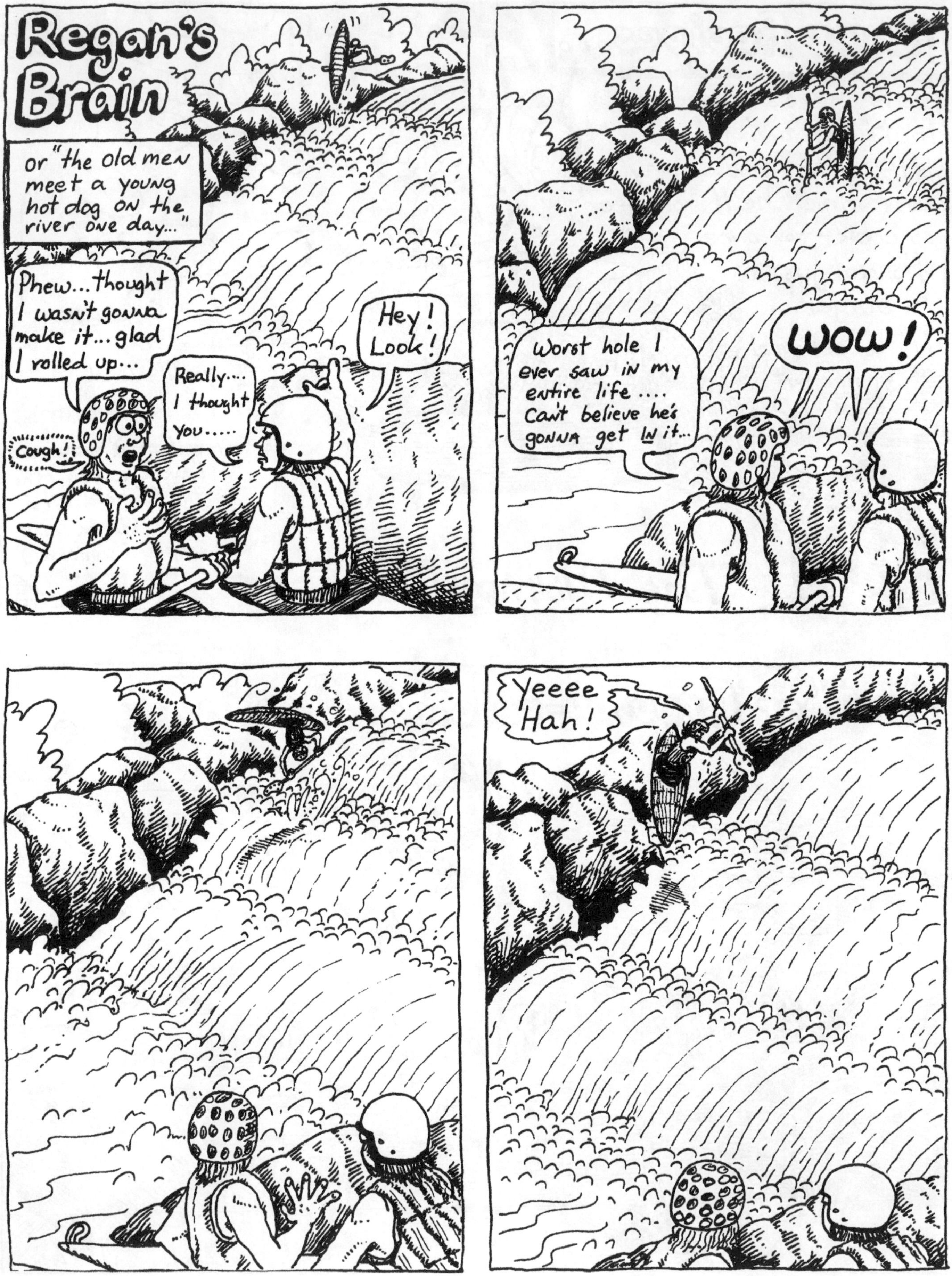

Regan's Brain
or "the old men meet a young hot dog on the river one day..."
Phew... thought I wasn't gonna make it... glad I rolled up...
Cough!
Really.... I thought you.....
Hey! Look!
Worst hole I ever saw in my entire life.... Can't believe he's gonna get IN it...
WOW!
Yeeee Hah!

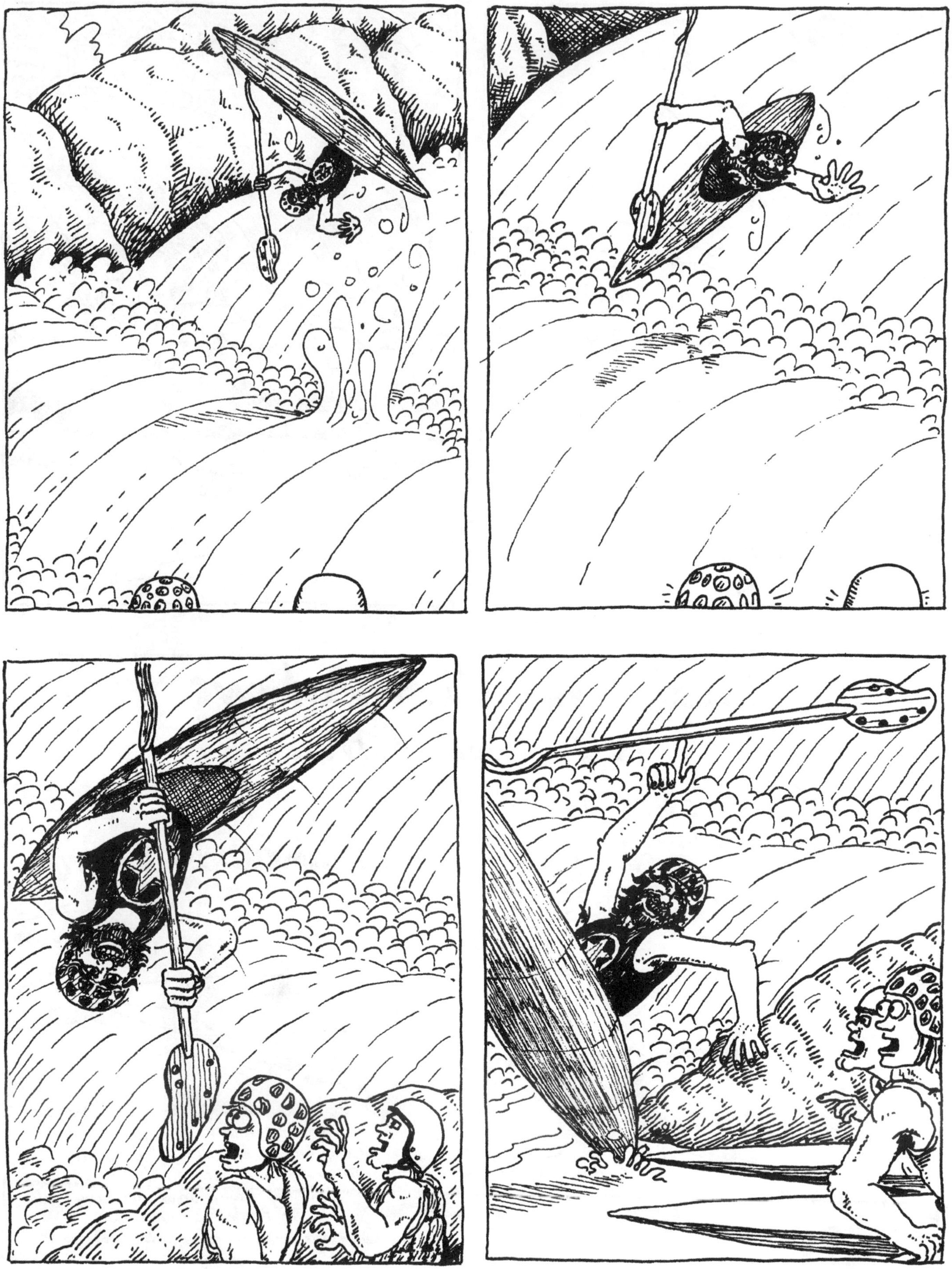

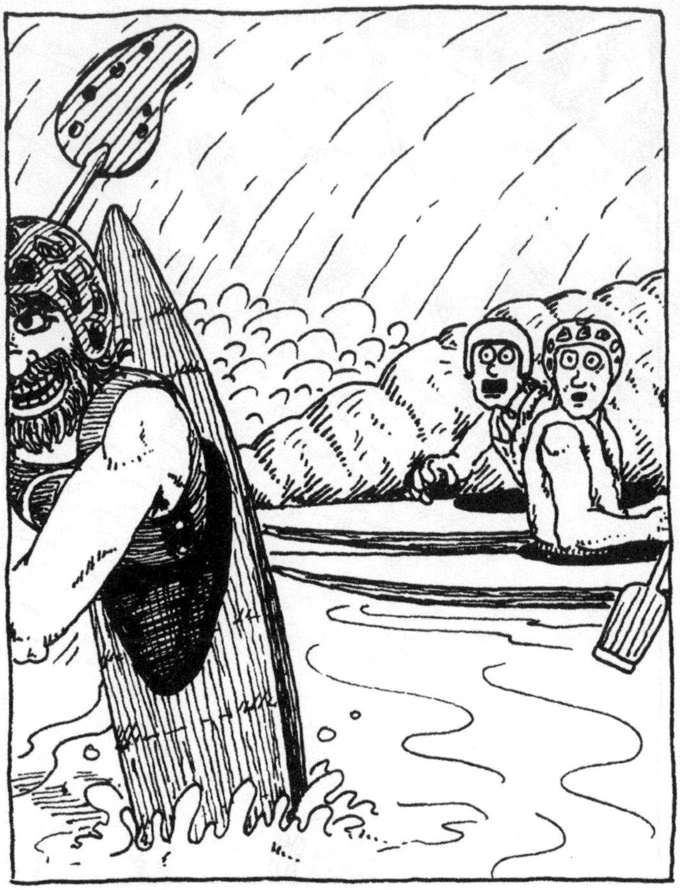

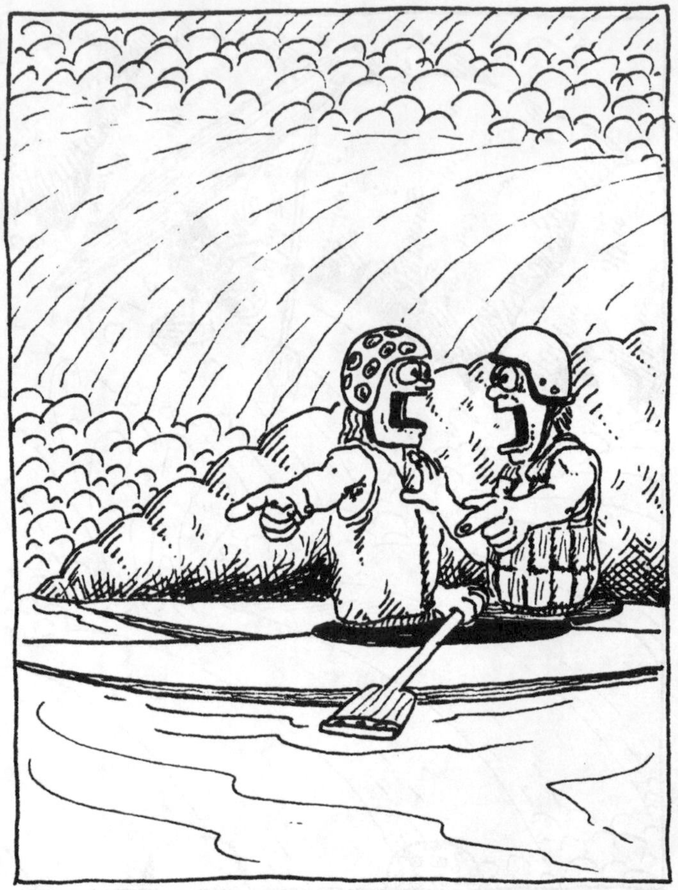

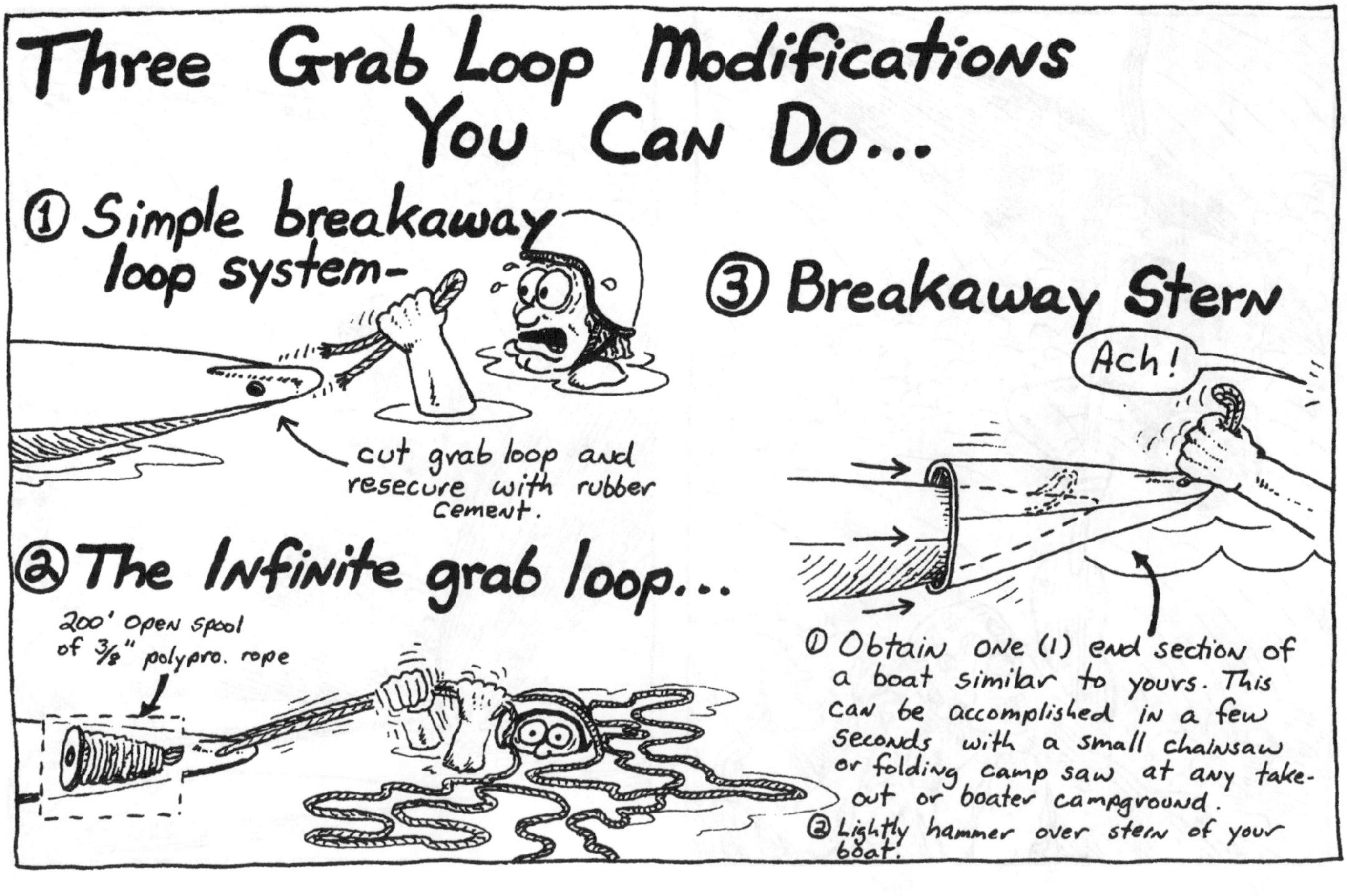
Three Grab Loop Modifications You Can Do...
① Simple breakaway loop system-
cut grab loop and resecure with rubber cement.
② The Infinite grab loop...
200' open spool of 3/8" polypro. rope
③ Breakaway Stern
Ach!
① Obtain one (1) end section of a boat similar to yours. This can be accomplished in a few seconds with a small chainsaw or folding camp saw at any take-out or boater campground.
② Lightly hammer over stern of your boat.

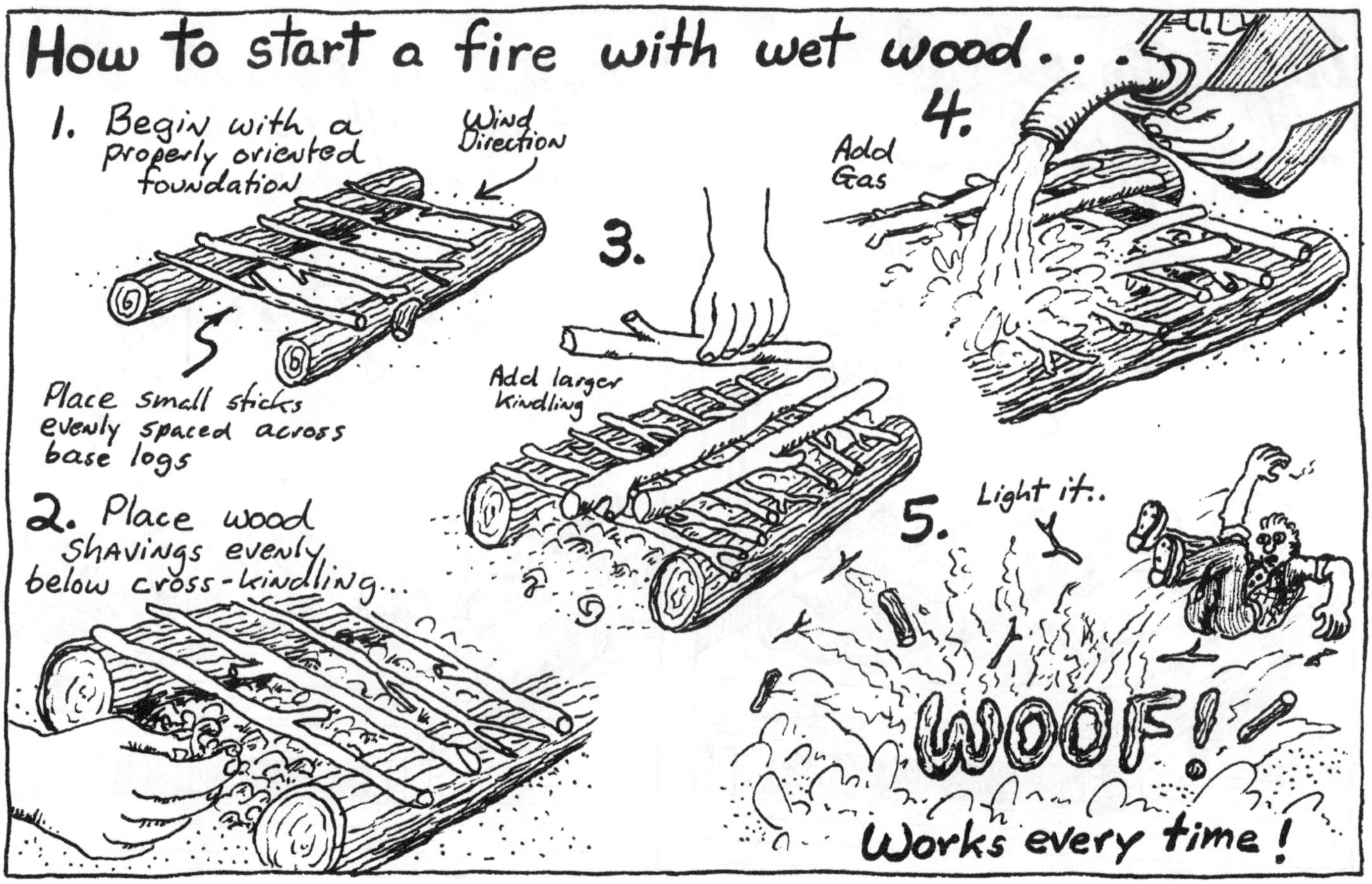
How to start a fire with wet wood...
1. Begin with a properly oriented foundation
Wind Direction
Place small sticks evenly spaced across base logs
2. Place wood shavings evenly below cross-kindling...
3.
Add larger Kindling
4.
Add Gas
5. Light it..
WOOF!
Works every time!

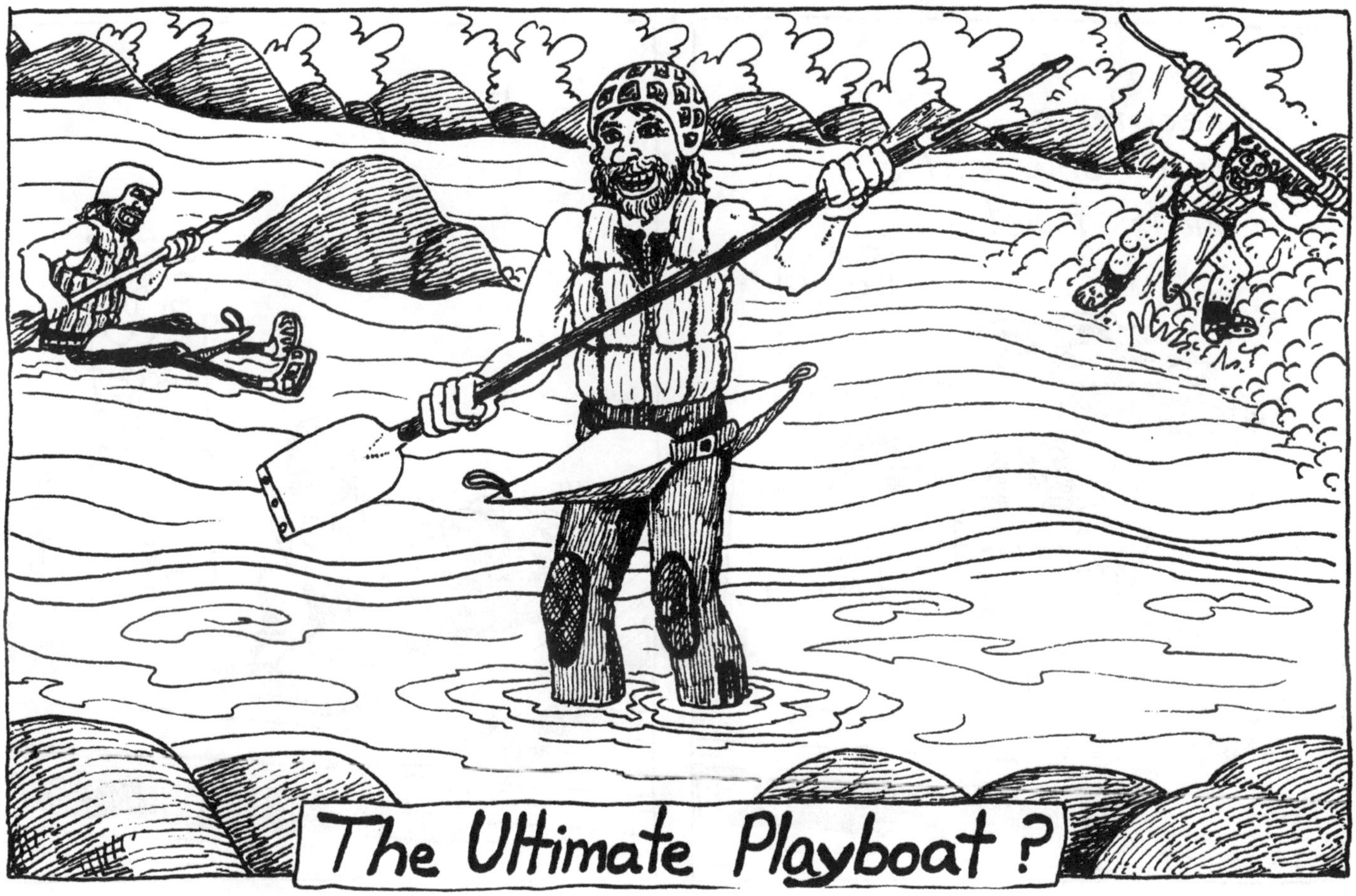
The Ultimate Playboat?

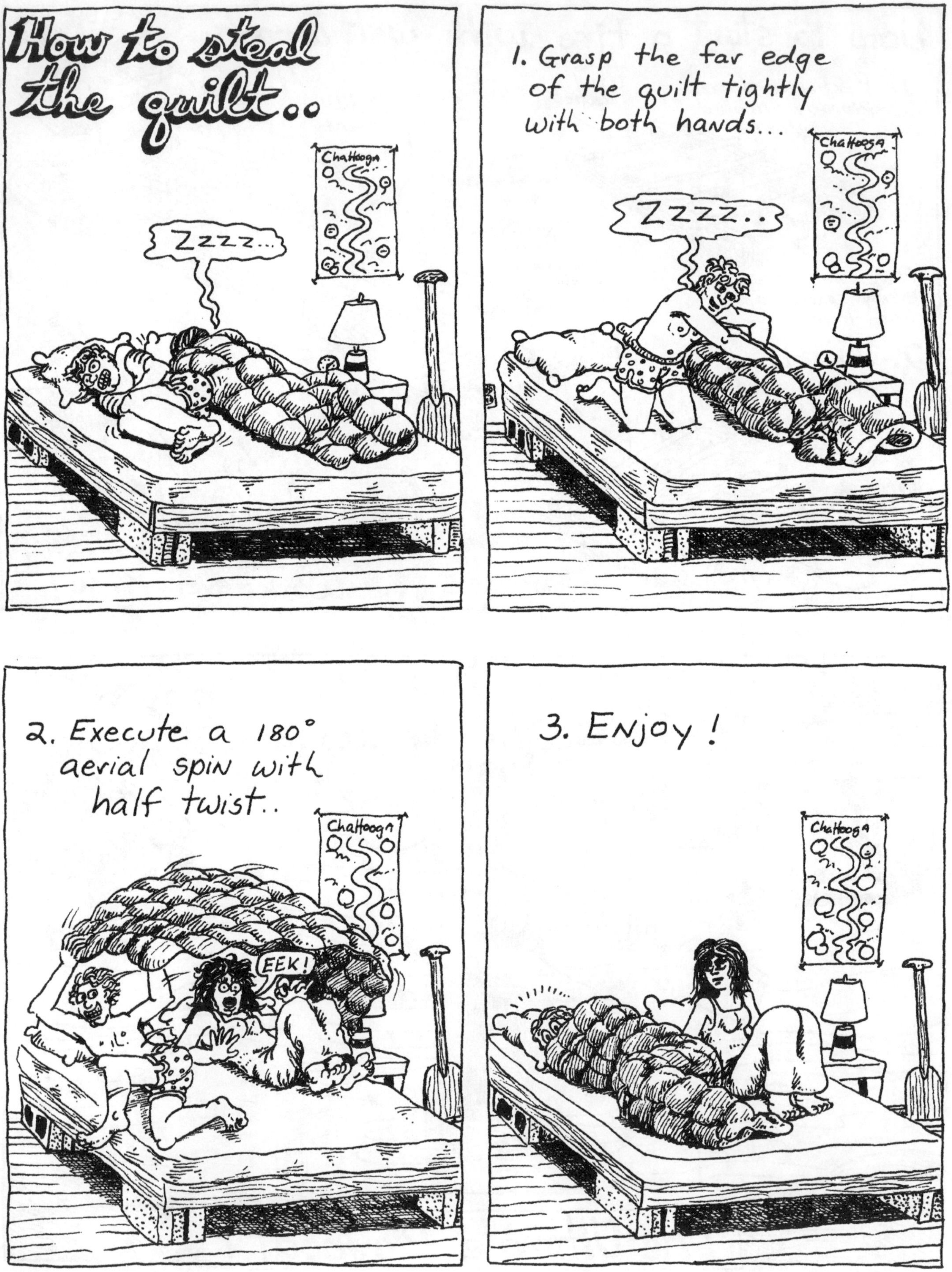
How to steal the quilt..
Chattooga
Zzzz...
1. Grasp the far edge of the quilt tightly with both hands...
Chattooga
Zzzz..
2. Execute a 180° aerial spin with half twist..
Chattooga
EEK!
3. Enjoy!
Chattooga

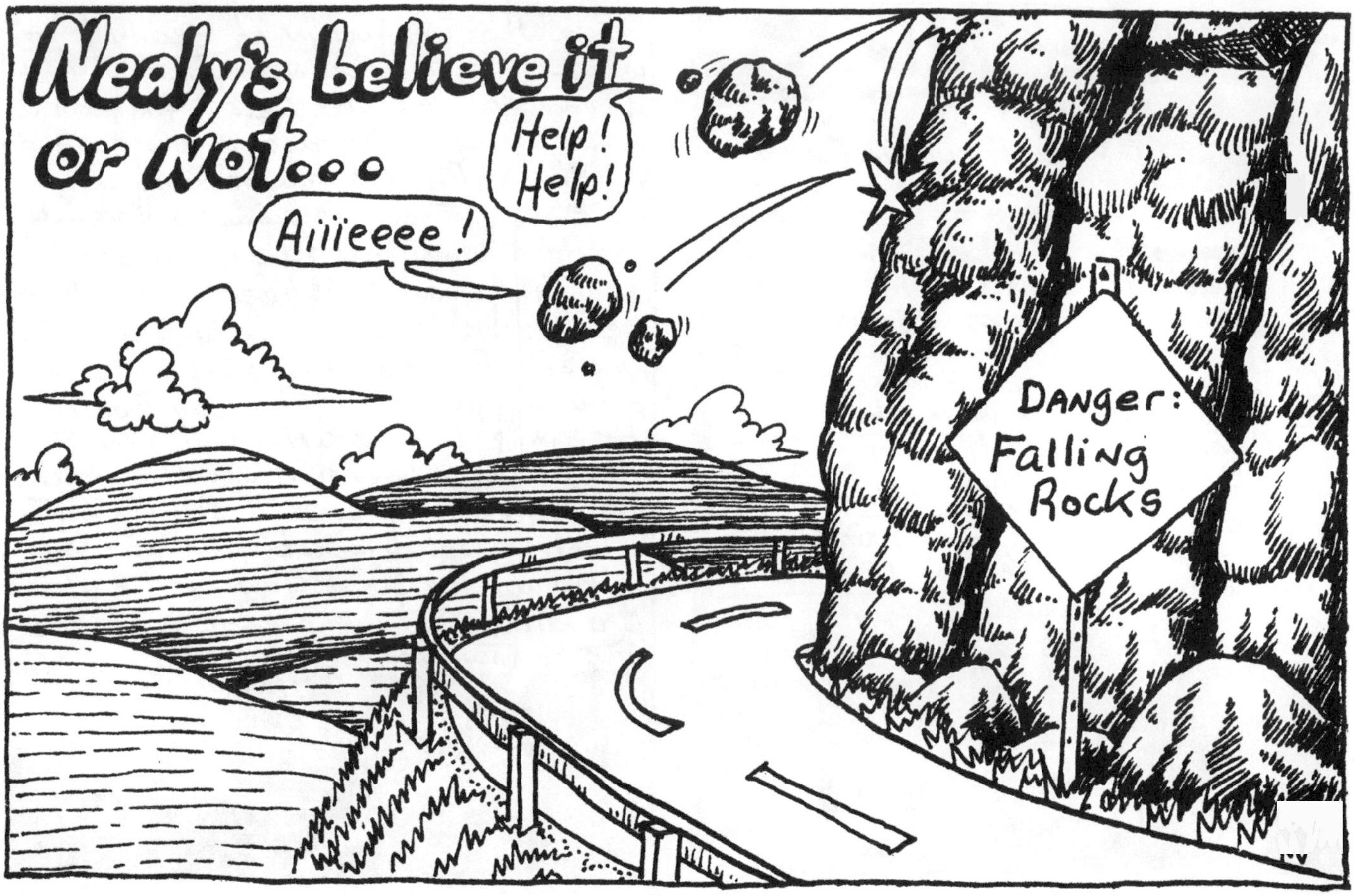
Nealy's believe it or Not...
Help! Help!
Aiiieeee!
Danger: Falling Rocks

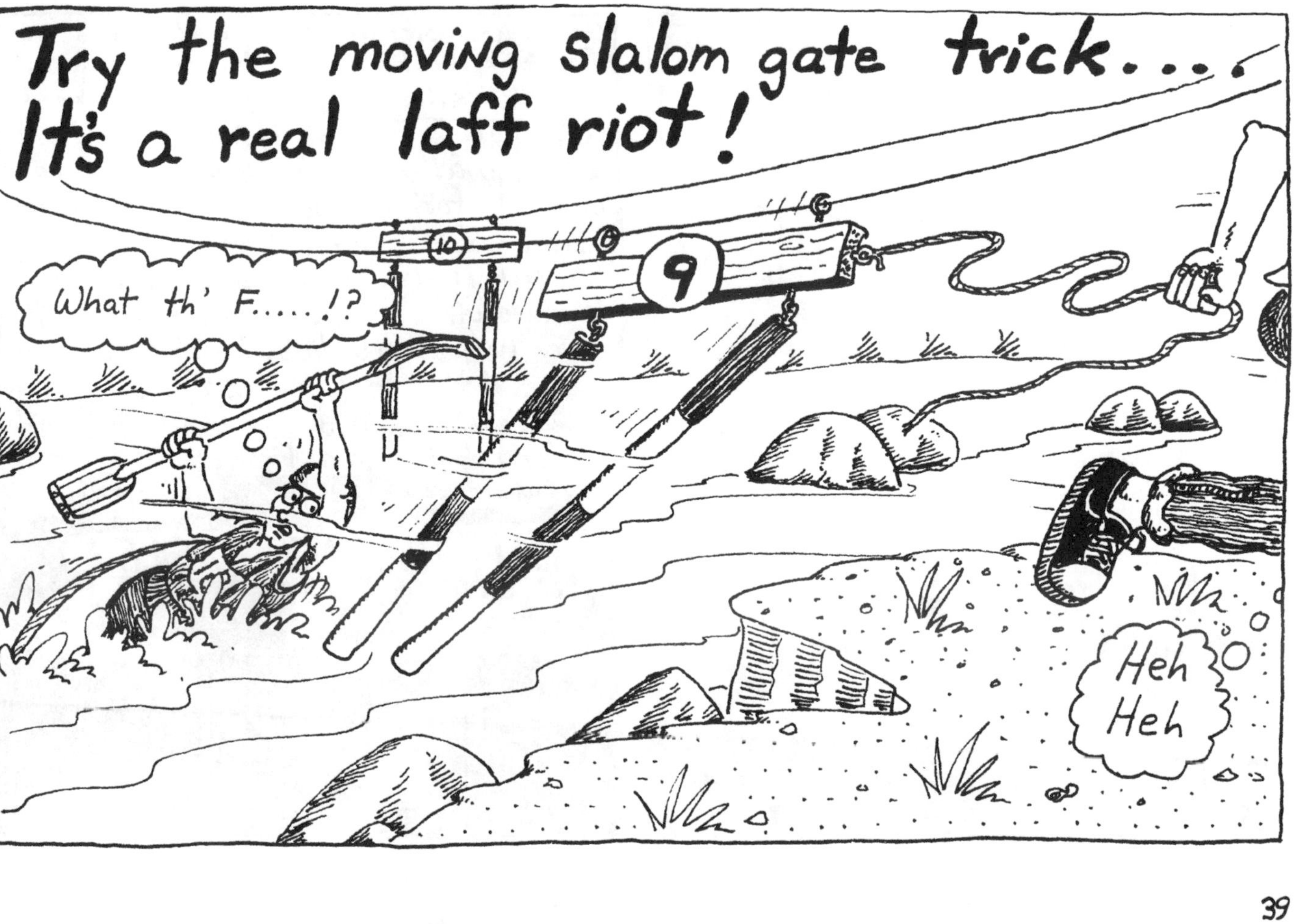
Try the moving slalom gate trick... It's a real laff riot!
10
9
What th' F.....!?
Heh Heh

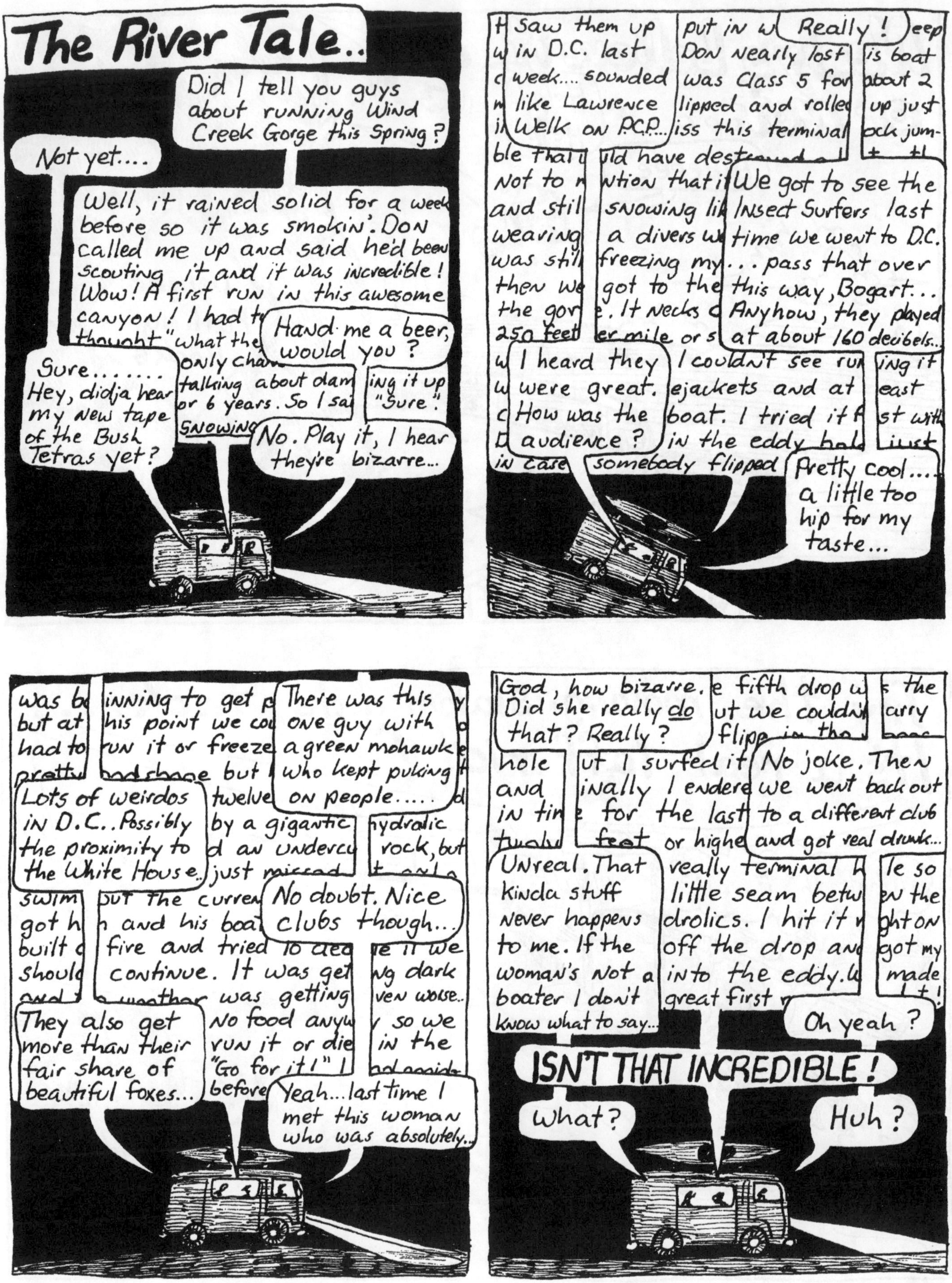
The River Tale..
Did I tell you guys about running Wind Creek Gorge this Spring?
Not yet....
Well, it rained solid for a week before so it was smokin'. DON called me up and said he'd been scouting it and it was incredible! Wow! A first run in this awesome canyon!
Hand me a beer, would you?
Sure....... Hey, didja hear my new tape of the Bush Tetras yet?
No. Play it, I hear they're bizarre...
Saw them up in D.C. last week.... sounded like Lawrence Welk on P.C.P....
Really!
We got to see the Insect Surfers last time we went to D.C. ... pass that over this way, Bogart... Anyhow, they played at about 160 decibels...
I heard they were great. How was the audience?
Pretty cool.... a little too hip for my taste...
There was this one guy with a green mohawk who kept puking on people.....
Lots of weirdos in D.C.. Possibly the proximity to the White House..
No doubt. Nice clubs though...
They also get more than their fair share of beautiful foxes...
Yeah... last time I met this woman who was absolutely...
God, how bizarre. Did she really do that? Really?
No joke. Then we went back out to a different club and got real drunk...
Unreal. That kinda stuff never happens to me. If the woman's not a boater I don't know what to say...
Oh yeah?
ISN'T THAT INCREDIBLE!
What?
Huh?

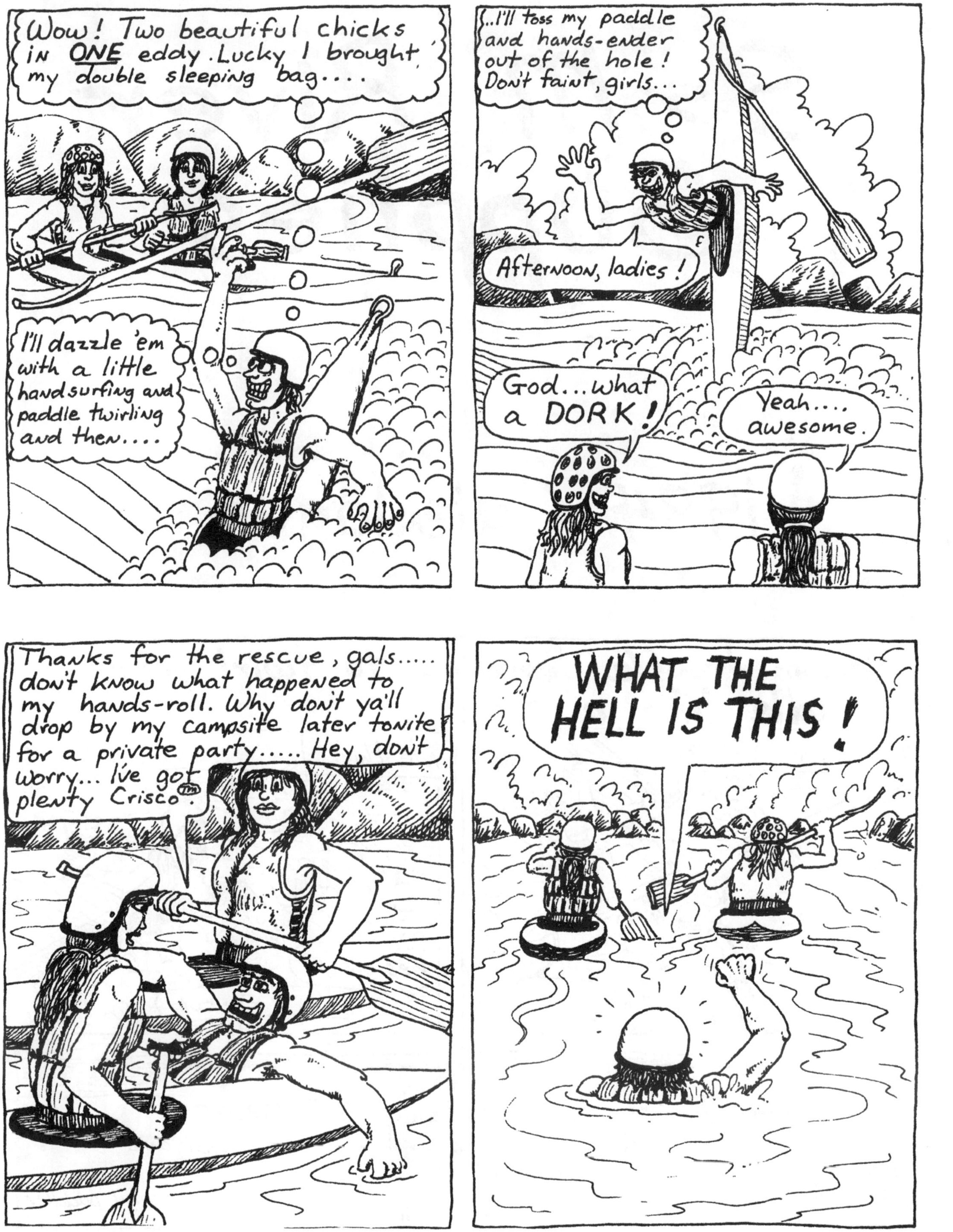
Wow! Two beautiful chicks in ONE eddy. Lucky I brought my double sleeping bag....
I'll dazzle 'em with a little handsurfing and paddle twirling and then....
...I'll toss my paddle and hands-ender out of the hole! Don't faint, girls...
Afternoon, ladies!
God...what a DORK!
Yeah.... awesome.
Thanks for the rescue, gals..... don't know what happened to my hands-roll. Why don't ya'll drop by my campsite later tonite for a private party..... Hey, don't worry... I've got plenty Crisco™.
WHAT THE HELL IS THIS!

S&M River Supplies

1984 Catalogue

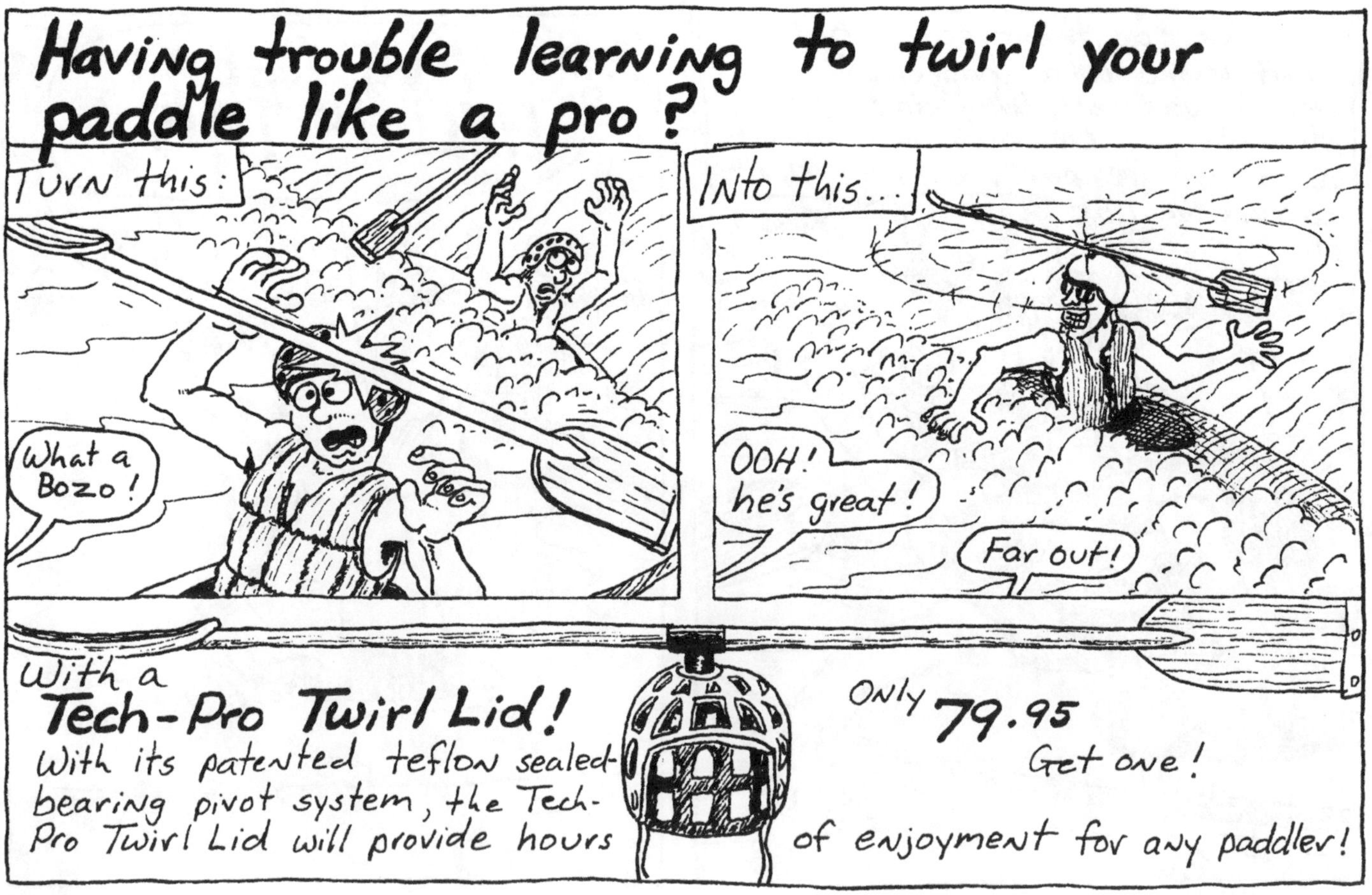

Having trouble learning to twirl your paddle like a pro?
Turn this:
What a Bozo!
Into this...
OOH! he's great!
Far out!
With a
Tech-Pro Twirl Lid!
With its patented teflon sealed-bearing pivot system, the Tech-Pro Twirl Lid will provide hours of enjoyment for any paddler!
Only 79.95
Get one!

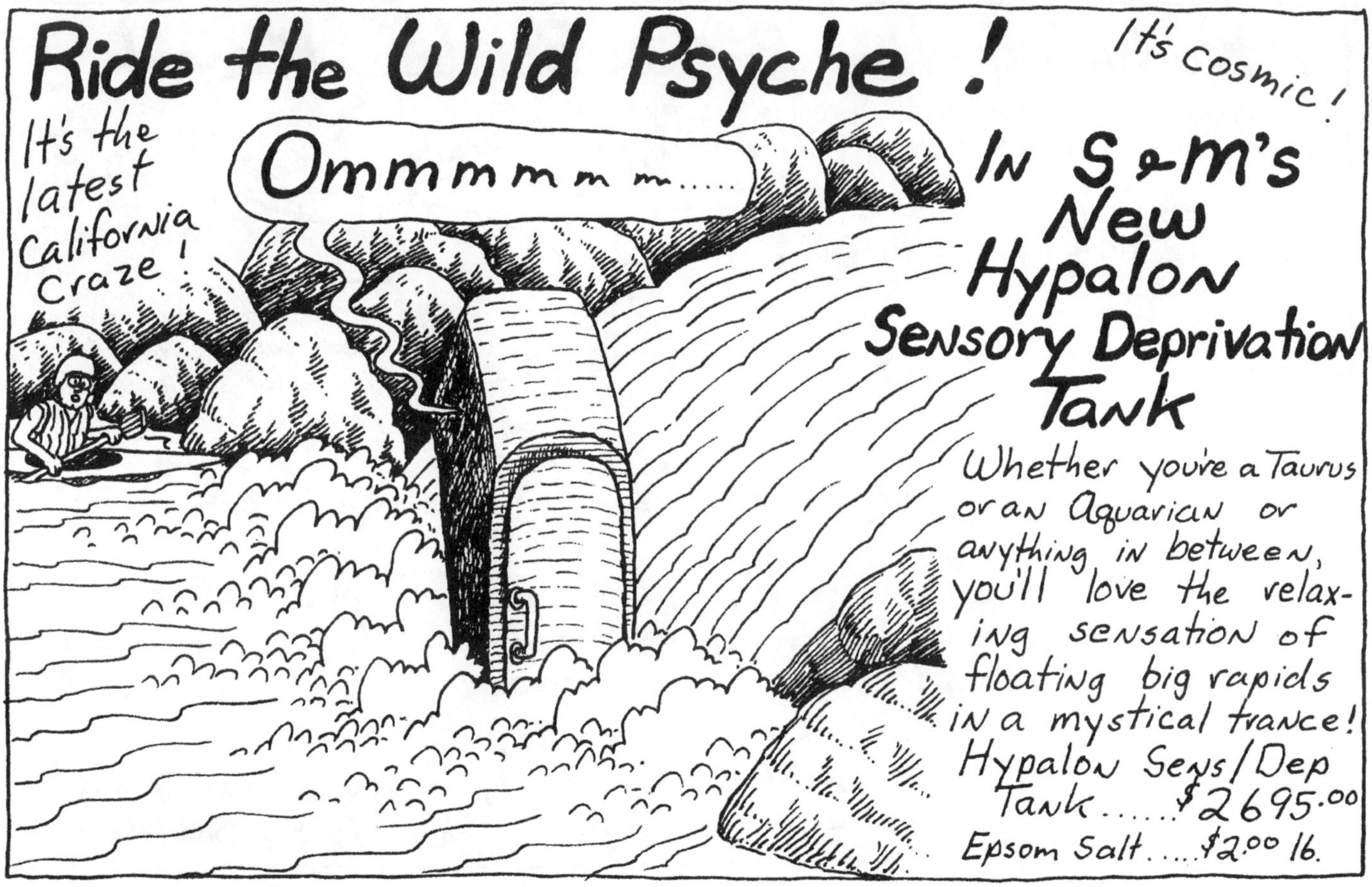
Ride the Wild Psyche!
It's cosmic!
It's the latest California craze!
Ommmmmm......
In S&M's New Hypalon Sensory Deprivation Tank
Whether you're a Taurus or an Aquarian or anything in between, you'll love the relaxing sensation of floating big rapids in a mystical trance!
Hypalon Sens/Dep Tank..... $2695.00
Epsom Salt.... $2.00 lb.

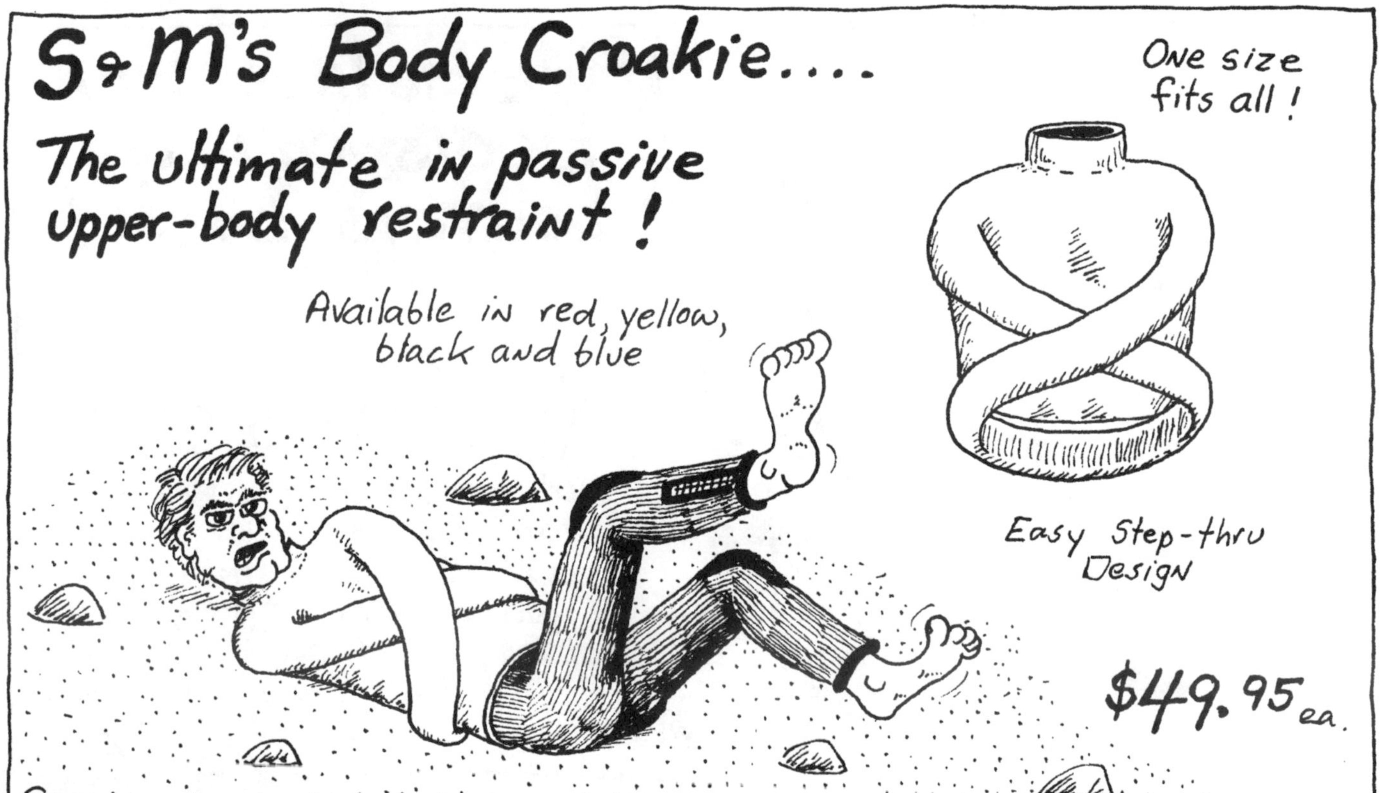
S&M's Body Croakie....
One size fits all!
The ultimate in passive upper-body restraint!
Available in red, yellow, black and blue
Easy Step-thru Design
$49.95 ea.
Coming soon: Wrist and ankle croakies...

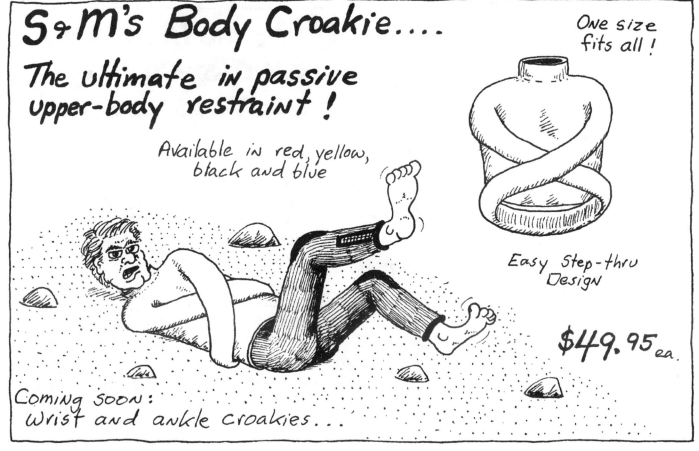

Introducing the B-52 Bomber Kayak!

Designed by America's foremost authority on existential boat design, W. Nealy...

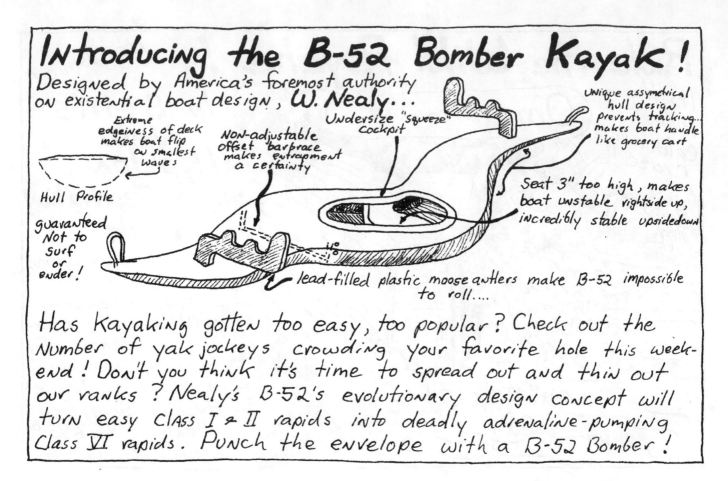

Extreme edgeiness of deck makes boat flip on smallest waves

Hull Profile

guaranteed Not to surf or ender!

NON-adjustable offset barbrace makes entrapment a certainty

Undersize "squeeze" Cockpit

Unique assymetical hull design prevents tracking... makes boat handle like grocery cart

Seat 3" too high, makes boat unstable rightside up, incredibly stable upsidedown

lead-filled plastic moose antlers make B-52 impossible to roll....

Has kayaking gotten too easy, too popular? Check out the Number of yak jockeys crowding your favorite hole this weekend! Don't you think it's time to spread out and thin out our ranks? Nealy's B-52's evolutionary design concept will turn easy Class I & II rapids into deadly adrenaline-pumping Class VI rapids. Punch the envelope with a B-52 Bomber!

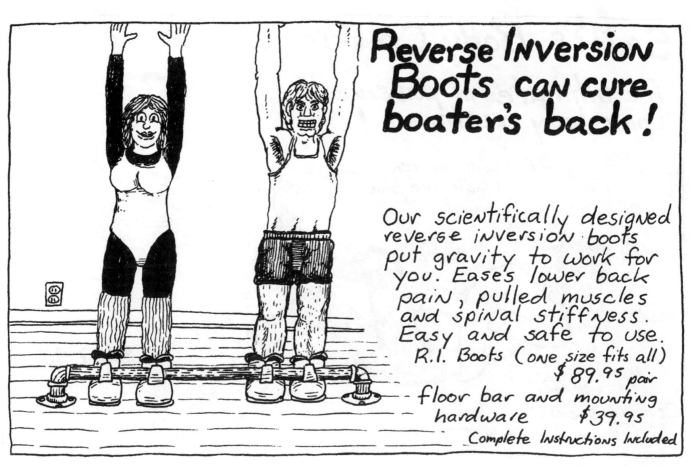

Reverse INVERSION Boots can cure boater's back!

Our scientifically designed reverse inversion boots put gravity to work for you. Eases lower back pain, pulled muscles and spinal stiffness. Easy and safe to use.
R.I. Boots (one size fits all) $89.95 pair
- floor bar and mounting hardware $39.95

Complete Instructions Included

Don't let this happen to you!

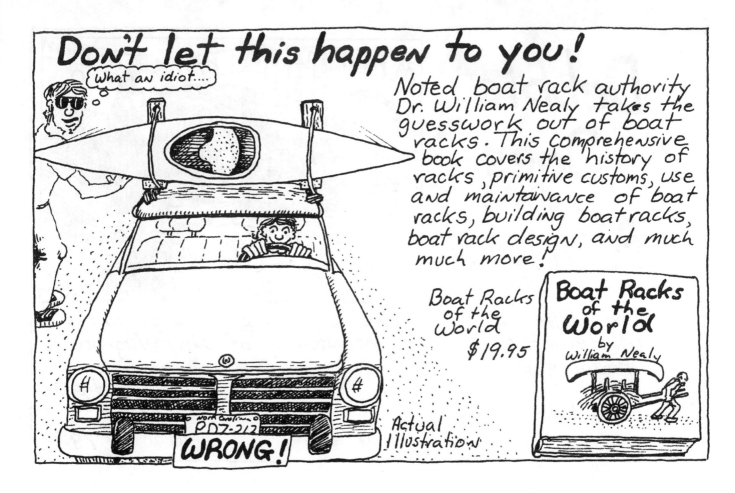

What an idiot....

WRONG!

Noted boat rack authority Dr. William Nealy takes the guesswork out of boat racks. This comprehensive book covers the history of racks, primitive customs, use and maintenance of boat racks, building boat racks, boat rack design, and much much more!

Boat Racks of the World $19.95

Boat Racks of the World by William Nealy

Actual Illustration

The S&M Campfire Songbook...

My Boat * (Nealy/Schlinkert/Wallace)

I've got sunshine on a cloudy day....
When it's cold outside I've got the month of May.....
(Chorus) I guess you'll say what can make me feel this way.....
my boat...... my boat...... my boat.........
talkin' 'bout my boat......... my boat!
oooo000 ooo000oooo (fade)
Moves so fast in the water the fish envy me......
I'm surfing bigger waves, baby, than old Waikiki.....
(Chorus)
I don't need no duct tape, got no busted seams.....
She's made of Kevlar......

*Sung to the tune of "My Girl" - Temptations

The kayak of my dreams...
(Chorus)
I've got dry feet on a rainy day....
In my cockpit it's the month of May..
It's such a dry boat
.... my boat! (fade out)
©1983 - Wet White Boys Music, Inc.

Plus much much more!
Here's what else you get.....
"Death Raft!"   "My Wave!"
                "We gotta get out of
"Hole Hog" "Punch Out   this hole"
            At Chili Bar"   "Proud
"Gimmie Kevlar"   C-boat"
                         "Knees of
"I did it my way"   Stone"
                         "Tequila!"
The S&M Campfire Songbook (160 pp)
shipping included............. $6.95

45

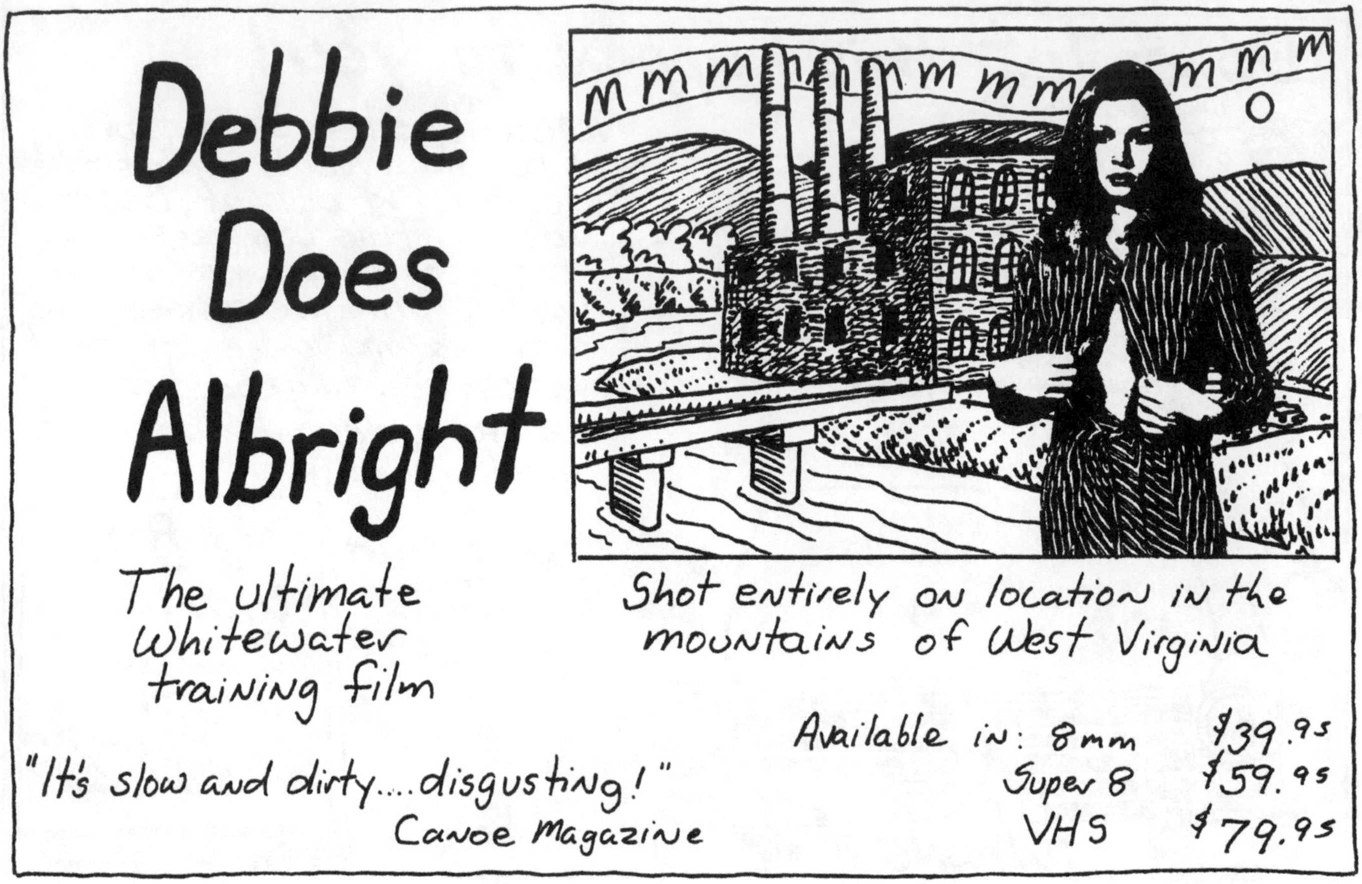
Debbie Does Albright
mmm mmm mmm
The ultimate Whitewater training film
Shot entirely on location in the mountains of West Virginia
Available in: 8mm $39.95
Super 8 $59.95
VHS $79.95
"It's slow and dirty.... disgusting!"
Canoe Magazine

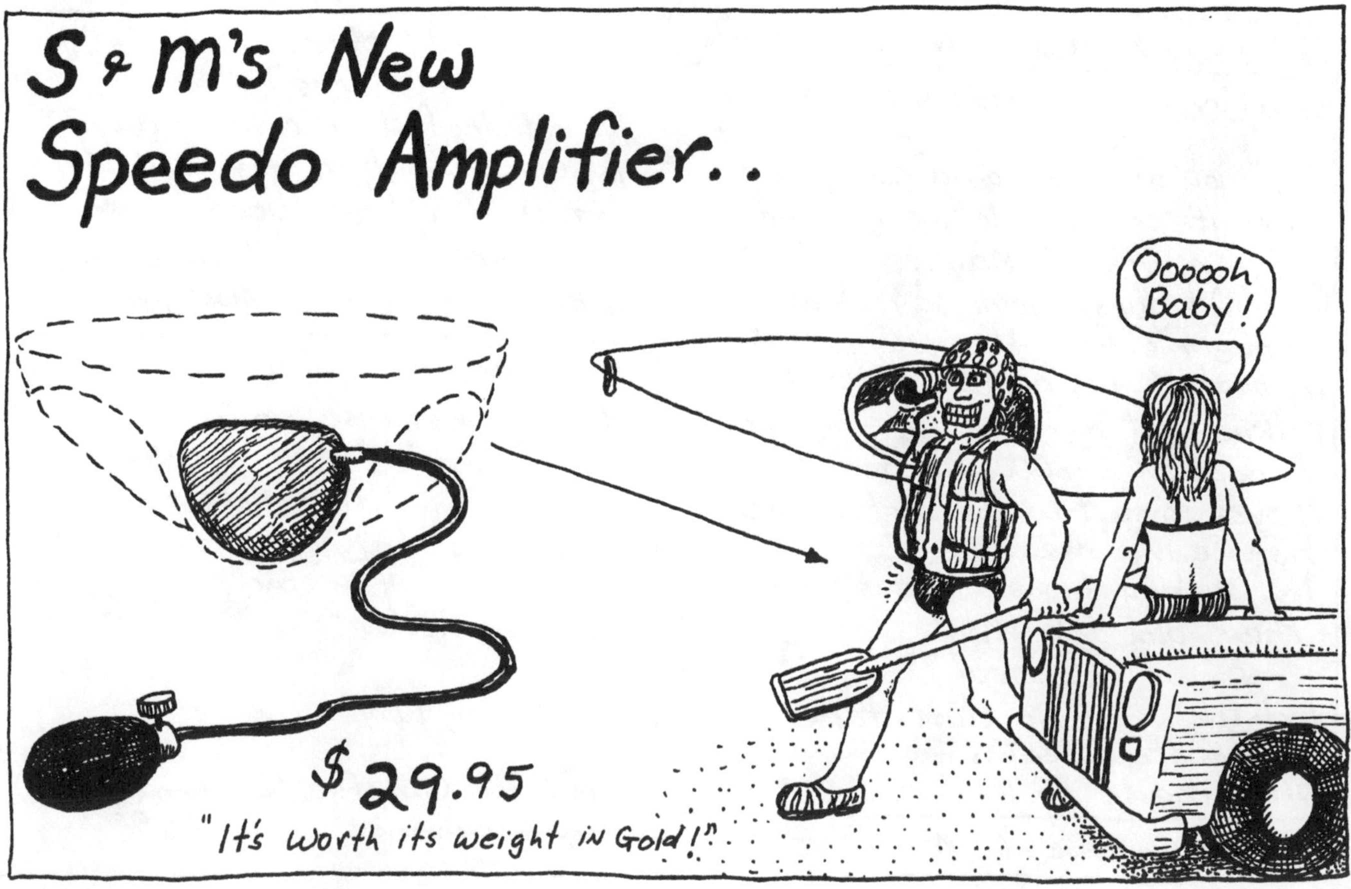
S & M's New Speedo Amplifier..
Oooooh Baby!
$29.95
"It's worth its weight in Gold!"

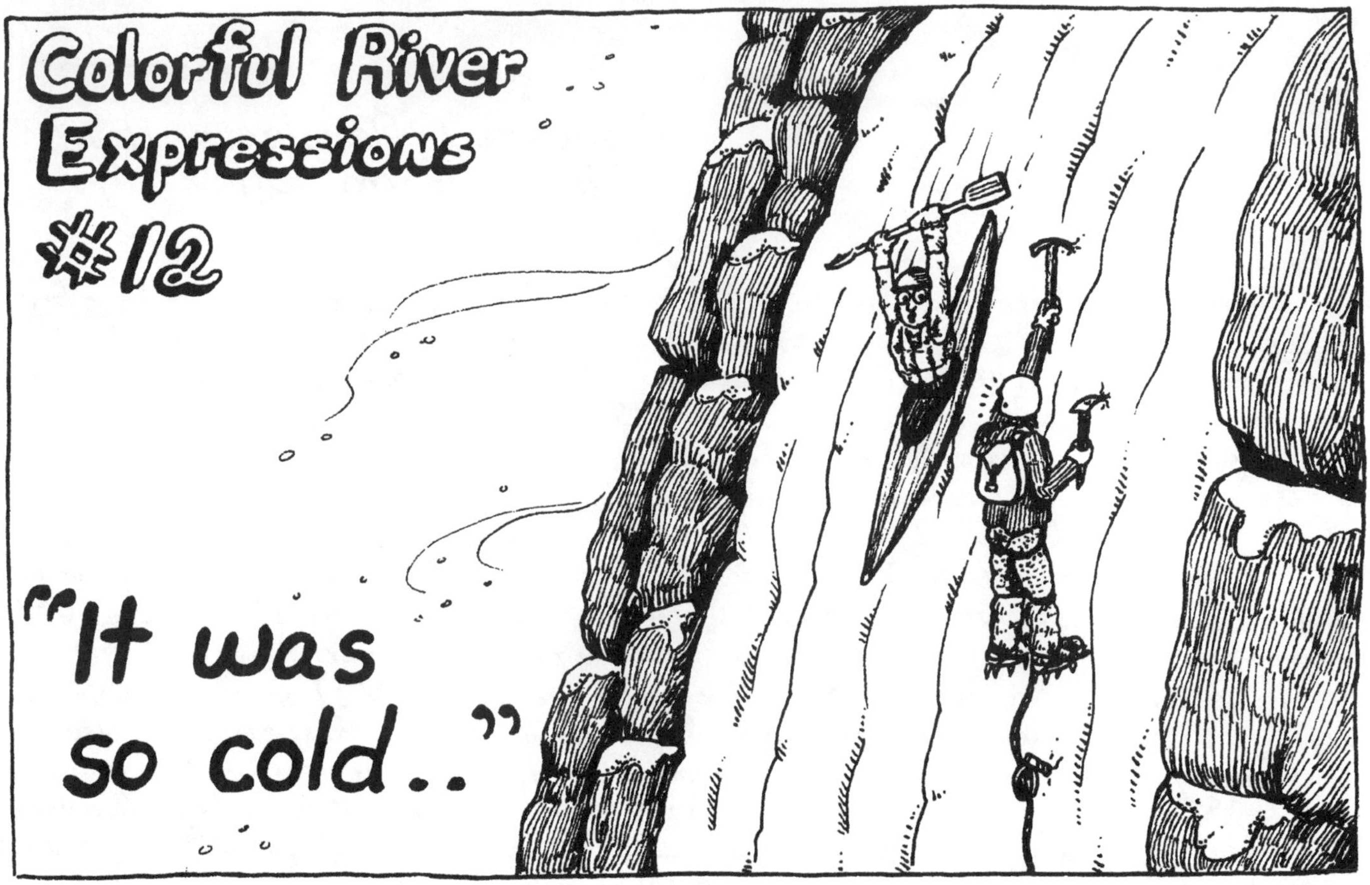

Colorful River Expressions #12
"It was so cold.."

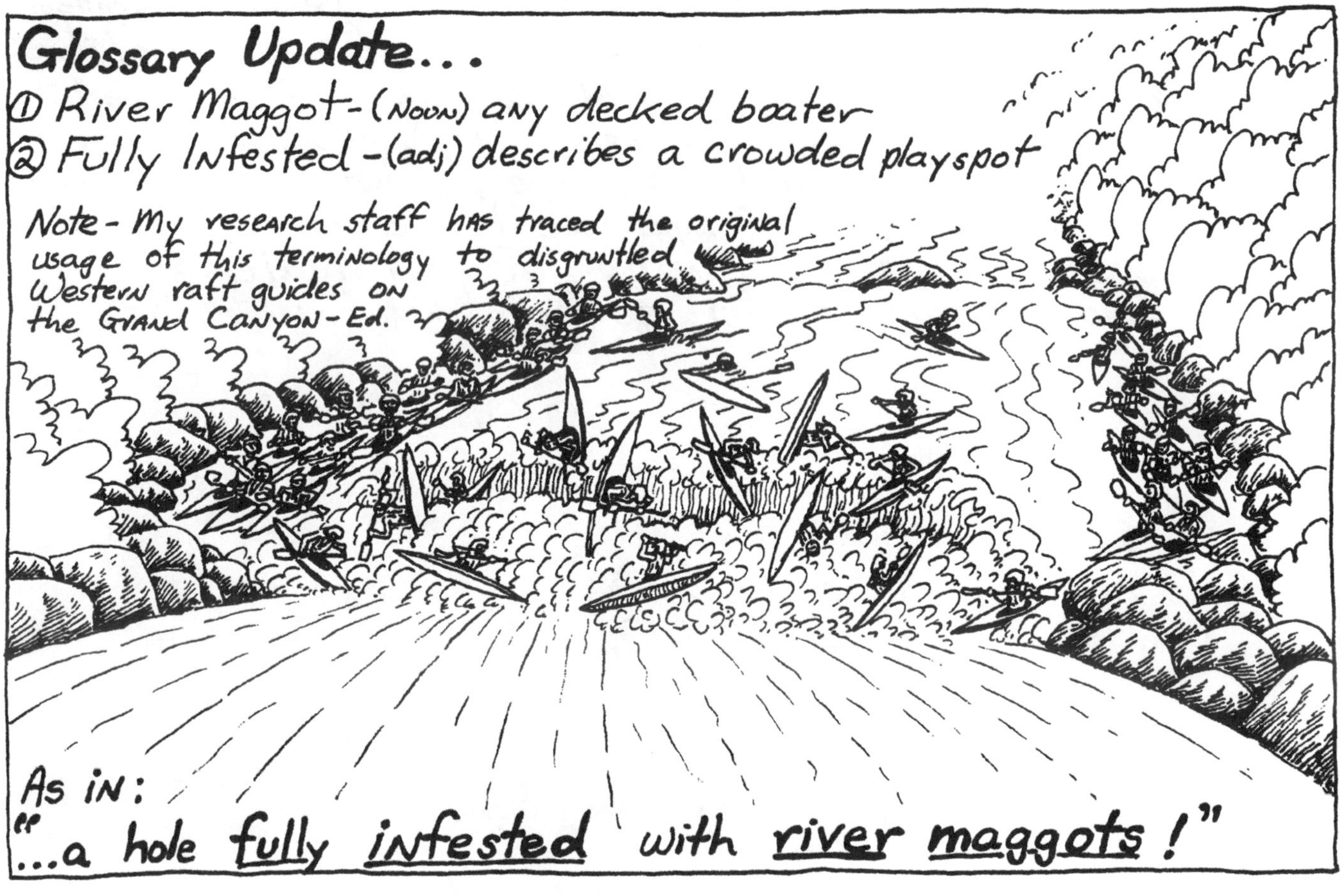

Glossary Update...
① River Maggot-(Noun) any decked boater
② Fully Infested-(adj) describes a crowded playspot
Note- My research staff has traced the original usage of this terminology to disgruntled Western raft guides on the Grand Canyon-Ed.
As in:
"...a hole fully infested with river maggots!"

William Nealy / S&m Products
Rt 3, Box 450
Hillsborough, N.C. 27278

Disgusted Readers - Here's a handy form letter! ✓

Mr. Nealy;

I recently (bought, acquired, received [Circle one]) a copy of <u>Whitewater Tales of Terror</u>. It is the most (tasteless, sickening, disgusting, deplorable, awful, depraved, reprehensible, nauseating [Circle one]) collection of (sociopathic, sick, demented, offensive, onerous, obnoxious [Circle one]) so-called cartoon humor I have seen in (weeks, years, recently, my life [Circle one]).

As a (responsible, respected, revered [Circle one]) member of the paddling community, I (was, am [Circle one]) (shocked, sickened, disturbed, saddened [Circle one]) by your depiction of (paddlers, women boaters, equipment manufactures, boat designers, rafters, mountain people [Circle one]) as (inferior, mindless, drug-crazed, egotistical, other_____ [Circle one], (zombies, sex-objects, morons, cretins, automatons, sex perverts [Circle one]) !

It is too bad a few (irresponsible, deranged, sick [Circle one]) people like you are trying to ruin the sport of (canoeing, kayaking [Circle one]) for everyone else. If you really think paddlers are (stupid, silly, lemming-like, cosmically superfluous, boring, [Circle one]) why don't you take up (scubadiving, hanggliding, skydiving, triathalon, jogging, skiing, other_____ [Circle one]) and inflict your poor sense of humor on someone else for a change.

For your information, there are many people involved in whitewater sports who are not brain-damaged habitual drug-abusers like yourself. I myself am (a, an [Circle one]) (expert canoeist, expert kayaker, certified canoe instuctor, canoe livery owner, outfitter, boat designer, equipment manufacturer, [Circle one]) with many years of experience both on and off rivers and I fail to see the humor in any of your material.

Why don't you (grow up, quit drawing, f**k off [Circle one]) !

Yours,

P.S.- (I want my money back!)
(I'm suing you for libel!) [Circle one]

48

ABOUT THE AUTHOR

William "Not Bill" Nealy was a wild, gentle, brilliant artist and creator turned cult hero who wrote 10 books for Menasha Ridge Press from 1982 to 2000. William shared his hard-won "crash-and-learn" experiences through humorous hand-drawn cartoons and illustrated river maps that enabled generations to follow in his footsteps. His subjects included paddling, mountain biking, skiing, and inline skating. His hand-drawn, poster-size river maps of the Nantahala, Ocoee, Chattooga, Gauley, Youghiogheny, and several other rivers are still sought after and in use today.

William was born in Birmingham, Alabama. He and his wife, Holly Wallace, spent their adult years in a home William built in the woods on the outskirts of Chapel Hill, North Carolina, along with an assortment of dogs, lizards, pigs, snakes, turtles, and amphibians. William died in 2001.

His longtime friend and publisher, Bob Sehlinger, wrote: "When William Nealy died in 2001, paddling lost its poet laureate, one of its best teachers, and its greatest icon. William was arguably the best-known ambassador of whitewater sport, entertaining and instructing hundreds of thousands of paddlers through his illustrated books, including the classics: *Whitewater Home Companion Volumes I and II, Whitewater Tales of Terror, Kayaks to Hell,* and his best-known work, *Kayak,* which combined expert paddling instruction with artful caricatures and parodies of the whitewater community itself."

You can learn more about William, his art, and his many books at thewilliamnealy.com.

photo: MAGPIE

Printed in the USA
CPSIA information can be obtained
at www.ICGtesting.com
JSHW061121250823
47224JS00002B/6

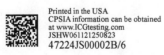

9 781634 043724